MW01166207

Japan

The Ultimate Japan Travel Guide By A Traveler For A Traveler

The Best Travel Tips: Where To Go, What To See And Much More

SECOND EDITION

Table of Contents

Why Lost Travelers Guides?

First, we want to wish you an amazing time in Japan when you plan to visit. Also we would like to thank you and congratulate you for downloading our travel guide, *"Japan; The Ultimate Japan Travel Guide By A Traveler For A Traveler"*.

Allow us to explain our beginnings, and the reason we created Lost Travelers. Lost Travelers was created due to one simple problem that other guides on the market did not solve; loss of time. Considering it's the 21st century and everything is available online, why do we still purchase guidebooks? To save us time! That's right.

Since the goal is to be efficient and save time, we did not understand why there are several guidebooks on the market that are of 500 to 1000 page' long. We do not believe one needs that much bluff to get an overview of the location and some remarkable suggestions. Considering many guidebooks on the market are filled with "suggestions" that were sponsored for, we have decided to take a different approach and provide our travelers with an honest opinion and decline any sort of sponsorship. This simply allows us to cut off any nonsense and create our guides the Lost Travelers style.

Our mission is simple; to create an easy to follow guide book that outlines the best of activities to do in our limited time at the destination. This easily saves you your most valuable asset; your time. You no longer need to spend hours looking through a massive book, or spend hours searching for information on the internet as we have completed the whole process for you. The best part is we provide you our e-guides for one third the price of the leading brand, and our paper copy for only half the price.

Thanks again for choosing us, we hope you enjoy!

© **Copyright 2016 by Seven Tree Group Inc. - All rights reserved.**

This document is geared towards providing exact and reliable information in regards to the topic and issue covered. The publication is sold with the idea that the publisher is not required to render accounting, officially permitted, or otherwise, qualified services. If advice is necessary, legal or professional, a practiced individual in the profession should be ordered.

- From a Declaration of Principles which was accepted and approved equally by a Committee of the American Bar Association and a Committee of Publishers and Associations.

In no way is it legal to reproduce, duplicate, or transmit any part of this document in either electronic means or in printed format. Recording of this publication is strictly prohibited and any storage of this document is not allowed unless with written permission from the publisher. All rights reserved.

The information provided herein is stated to be truthful and consistent, in that any liability, in terms of inattention or otherwise, by any usage or abuse of any policies, processes, or directions contained within is the solitary and utter responsibility of the recipient reader. Under no circumstances will any legal responsibility or blame be held against the publisher for any reparation, damages, or monetary loss due to the information herein, either directly or indirectly.

Respective authors own all copyrights not held by the publisher.

The information herein is offered for informational purposes solely, and is universal as so. The presentation of the information is without contract or any type of guarantee assurance.

The trademarks that are used are without any consent, and the publication of the trademark is without permission or backing by the trademark owner. All trademarks and brands within this book are for clarifying purposes only and are the owned by the owners themselves, not affiliated with this document.

Chapter 1: Get to Know Japan

So, what inspired you to want to go to Japan? Is it in the Japanese pop culture that Western countries have grown to be so fond of, such as the anime that you used to watch as a kid (or maybe keep on watching until now)? Is it the cool, futuristic inventions in robotics that the Japanese are always able to come up with? Is it the ancient culture, of samurai, Shintoism, tea ceremonies, flower arrangements, bonsai, and geisha? Do you find the lifestyle in Tokyo captivating and motivating? Or maybe you are simply a curious traveler who wants to see the world and appreciate its wonders. Whatever your reasons may be, it cannot be denied that Japan has so much to offer.

Japan is an East Asian country commonly referred to as the *Land of the Rising Sun*, and its locals call it *Nippon* or *Nihon* (formally *Nippon-koku* or *Nihon-koku*, both of which mean *State of Japan*). The locals call themselves *Nihonjin* and the Japanese language as *Nihongo*.

Brief History

While this serves only as a brief overview, it is nevertheless important to brush up on the important historical periods in order to gain appreciation for the places that you will visit as well as the culture of Japan.

You might already have an idea that Japan has a long and deeply interesting history. According to archaeologists, humans have been living in the island since the Upper Paleolithic Era. Much of its culture is influenced by Imperial China (including the writing system and Buddhism) and, later on, Western Europe, although Japanese culture in and of itself is distinct and rich.

The years between 710 and 784 marked the *Nara Period*, in which a solid Japanese state emerged. Japanese Buddhism heavily influenced the literature, architecture, and art during this time.

This was followed by the Heian Period, which fell between 794 and 1185. This time, indigenous Japanese culture became more significant, particularly in poetry and art. It is worth noting that the lyrics of *Kimigayo*, or the Japanese national anthem, was composed within this period.

The rise of the warrior class, or the *samurai*, immediately followed the Heian period. This is often referred to as the Kamakura period, which spanned from 1185 to 1333. The center of the country was in Kamakura, ruled by a samurai shogun named Minamoto no Yoritomo. Mongol invasions between 1274 and 1281 caused much distress to the shogunate, leading to it being overthrown by the Mongol Emperor, Go-Daigo. However, the samurai Ashikaga Takauji was able to defeat the Go-Daigo and establish his shogunate in Kyoto.

The rise of the Ashikaga shogunate also marked the beginning of the Muromachi Period, which fell between 1336 and 1573. It was during this time when Zen Buddhism became a central part of the Japanese culture. This later developed into the Higashiyama Culture, which continued on until the 16th century. The Higashiyama Culture is still revered in modern-day Japan and across the globe, its main theme being *beauty in simplicity*. From this culture, the *sumi-e* ink painting, *Noh* drama, *chadō* (Japanese tea ceremony) and *ikebana* (flower arranging) were conceptualized.

Unfortunately, the Ashikaga shogunate that proceeded after the reign of Ashikaga Takauji was unable to govern over the feudal lords, and in 1467, the civil war referred to as the Ōnin War started. This era is referred to as the Sengoku period, and it lasted for a hundred years.

Sometime in the 16th century, Portuguese traders and Jesuit missionaries were able to travel to Japan, opening up a cultural and commercial trade between Western Europe and Japan. A powerful feudal lord by the name of Oda Nobunaga was able to purchase European firearms, enabling him to conquer other feudal lords in an attempt to unify the country. This led to the transition from the Sengoku period to the Azuchi-Momoyama period between 1573 and 1603.

The year 1600 marked the Battle of Sekigahara, with Tokugawa Ieyasu as the shogun in 1603. The center of his shogunate was in Edo, which is now the modern-day Tokyo. During his rule, the shogunate established the *Laws for the Military Houses* or the *Buke shohatto*, a code of conduct meant to control the feudal lords. Eventually, in 1639, the shogunate launched the closed country policy, which lasted for over two hundred and fifty years. This was referred to as the Edo period, which lasted until 1868.

In the year 1854, the United States Navy under Commodore Matthew Perry forcibly opened Japan to the rest of the world via the Convention of Kanagawa, the first treaty between the Empire of Japan under the Tokugawa shogunate and the United States of America. This sparked the final years of the Edo period as well as the Tokugawa shogunate, leading to the establishment of the Meiji government, which adopted a more Western institution where military, political, and judicial aspects are concerned. During this time, the shogunate forces and the imperial nationalists were divided. It was also during this period when the Empire of Japan became an industrialized super power on a worldwide scale. Japan used its military to expand its power, eventually conquering Korea, Taiwan, and the south of Sakhalin.

At the beginning of the 20th century and during the World War I, Japan was able to further expand its territorial holdings. It was also around this time when the Meiji Emperor died and was succeeded by the Crown Prince Yoshihito. His reign opened the Taishō period, which took place briefly between 1912 and 1926.

In 1931, upon its occupation of Manchuria, Japan became the subject of international condemnation. In 1933, the government of Japan renounced itself from the League of Nations and in 1936, they joined forces with Nazi Germany by signing the Anti-Comintern Pact. This was followed in 1940 by the signing of the Tripartite Pact, and in 1941, Japan arranged for the Soviet-Japanese Neutrality Pact.

In 1937, Japan continued to invade the other parts of China, immediately bringing about the Second Sino-Japanese War, which began in 1937 and ended in 1945. These were dark years in World History, particularly when Japan conducted the Nanking Massacre, perpetrated by Prince Asaka of the Imperial Family. After the Empire of Japan occupied French Indochina in 1940, the United States forced an oil embargo. This was then followed by a series of attacks conducted by the Japanese forces on Pearl Harbor and the British forces in Hong Kong, Malaya, and Singapore. These compelled the US and the UK to join in World War II in the Pacific.

The chaos simmered down after the US launched atomic bombs to Nagasaki and Hiroshima and the Soviet invaded the state of Manchukuo under Japan, with Japan submitting to unconditional surrender on August 15, 1945. The Japanese empire was disarmed by the Allies of World War I, which became the foundation of the United Nations. The Allies forcibly sent ethnic Japanese in military camps and colonies back to the homeland.

Japan eventually implemented a new constitution in 1947, which placed emphasis on liberal democracy. In 1952, the Treaty of San Francisco was signed, concluding the Allied occupation in Japan. Four years later, Japan became a member of the United Nation. Since then, Japan continued to develop at an industrial scale until it became one of the most economically and technologically advanced countries in the world.

Modern-Day Japan

The government of modern Japan is a constitutional monarchy, wherein the Prime minister is the executive power and the Emperor is its head of state. The Parliament is called the Diet of Japan, and is composed of the House of Councilors as the upper house and the House of Representatives as the lower house.

Currently, Japan has an estimated population of over 127 million, with an astounding literacy rate of 99 percent and an average life expectancy (among females) of 84.5 years. Travelers in Japan are in awe of the mixture of the ancient culture with out-of-this-world modern advancements, particularly in robotics, nanotechnology, and chemical engineering.

Japan is not exempt from modern-world crises. In 2008, the country's economy suffered as an effect of the worldwide recession, partly due to the fact that 20 percent of its total manufacturing output is for export. Japan is also currently facing the *aging population* problem, with its birth rate being the second-lowest among the first world countries. This apparent lack in the next-generation workforce has led the country to import people from countries such as the Philippines, Indonesia, and Vietnam to temporarily work there.

Geography

Japan is composed of a group of islands and is located in the Western Pacific. It is located off the coast of China, with the Sea of Japan, and the East China Sea separating it from the continent of Asia.

There are six thousand small islands and four main ones, namely Kyushu, Hokkaido, Honshu, and Shikoku. Honshu (which translates to *Mainland* in Japanese) is the biggest island. To the north of Honshu is Hokkaido, to its west is Kyushu, and to its south-west is Shikoku.

Honshu is where Tokyo is located. It is where you can find the Imperial Palace and the center of the Japanese government. Yokohama, the second largest city, is also located in it.

Other big cities in Japan are: Nagoya, Osaka, Kyoto, Kobe, Hiroshima, Fukuoka, Kitakyushu, Sendai, Sapporo, and Nagasaki.

The center of Japan contains mountains, most of which are dormant and extinct volcanoes. The tallest and arguably the most beautiful one is Mt Fuji, which rises to 12,389 feet high. It may be due to the presence of these volcanoes that Japan experiences a series of earthquakes throughout the year.

Climate

Most of the time, the climate in Japan is temperate. The average temperature during the wintertime is 41.2 degrees F (or 5.1 degrees C) and for summer, 77.4 degrees F (or 25.2 degrees C). Of course, this also depends on the location. There are six principal climatic zones in Japan.

In the northernmost part is the Hokkaido zone, wherein people experience long and cold winter seasons and warm to cool summer ones, with a predominantly humid state overall.

The west coast of Honshu is the Sea of Japan zone where people experience heavy snow during the winter and cooler summers with the occasional extreme heat brought about by the down-slope *foehn* wind compared with the Pacific Ocean zone.

The Pacific Ocean zone has a humid sup-tropical climate, with mild winters and hot summers.

The Central Highland zone is where one can experience a generally humid climate, but with vast differences in temperature between days and nights and summer and winter seasons.

The Seto Inland Sea zone enjoys mild weather throughout the year due to it being sheltered by the Shikoku and Chugoku regions.

The Ryukyu Islands zone has a humid subtropic climate in the northern section and a more tropical rain forest climate in the south with very high precipitation. In this zone, the rains are heavy, the winters warm, and the summers hot.

Transportation

There are two main international airports in Japan: Narita Airport in Tokyo and Kansai Airport in Osaka. Other airports are the Fukuoka Airport, which connects flights mostly to Korea and China, Haneda Airport (in Tokyo) and Central Kansai Airport (in Nagoya). Japan has two leading airlines, Japan Airlines (JAL) and All Nippon Airways (ANA).

Travelers on a budget can save a lot on airfare if they book flights in the off-peak season (ideally between late autumn and early Spring, excluding the winter and New Year holiday season). Those who want to take part in the festivities should book well in advance, particularly around April 29 to May 5 and mid-August, as these dates hold the most important holidays in Japan.

For those planning to tour across Japan, it is usually more practical to get domestic air discounts, such as Star Alliance Japan Pass and Japan Airlines' *OneWorld Yokoso Visit Japan Fare*. Domestic flights can go as low as 112 USD. Another option is to take the Shinkansen or bullet train, but this can be more expensive than domestic flights.

One thing to remember on arriving at the airport is that the taxis are extremely expensive (at about 200 USD or more if you are going to travel from Narita Airport to Tokyo). What you can do instead is to take the bus or railway. *Limousine Buses* in Tokyo, for instance, can bring you to your hotel or to train stations for approximately 32 USD.

Keisei Line (railway) offers a trip to central Tokyo for even lower rates (approximately 14 USD), but be prepared for a longer trip. Nevertheless, you should highly consider getting a Japan Rail Pass (which can be availed by those on a tourist visa) before you go to Japan so that you can enjoy unlimited rides for up to three weeks (a 1-week pass is about 300 USD for regular cars and 415 USD for green cars, or the luxury car trains). The Tokyo subway is another way to get around the city, and is quite cheap at 1.71 USD per trip.

Bicycles can be rented for one whole day for less than 10 USD, and these are widely available near most train stations. It is a simple, inexpensive and highly convenient way to go around the city. Unless it's raining, of course.

As with any other trip to a foreign place, you should always carry an updated map with you.

Culture

The culture of the Japanese is rich and vast, albeit difficult to describe, and is often the main reason why people want to visit this country in the first place. Its modern-day culture can best be described as a hybrid one and to experience it deeply, you must immerse yourself into the language, art, and its other traditional and modern aspects.

The language of Japan has a pitch-accent system, with dialects varying in terms of accent. The standard Japanese accent is called the Tokyo Yamanote dialect, which you can hear in broadcasting shows. The written language is composed of three distinct scripts, namely hiragana, katakana, and kanji. Hiragana is a derivation of the Chinese cursive script, while katakana is the shorthand form derived from Chinese characters, and kanji evolved from the logographic system of China. You will also notice the use of the Latin alphabet in modern Japan, the symbols of which the Japanese call *rōmaji*. As for numbers, you will notice the use of both Sino-Japanese numerals and Hindu-Arabic numerals.

Calligraphy, or *shodou* to the locals, is a highly valuable art form in Japan. High quality handwriting is revered, and the unique brush strokes of celebrities are highly valuable to their fans. Many travelers love to enroll in a short calligraphy workshop, especially those who wish to learn *kanji*.

Japan is also home to the art of growing *bonsai,* or miniaturizing a plant, typically a pine tree. Flower arranging (*ikebana*) is an important part of their culture as well, and Japanese ladies are expected in their society to know how to execute this art.

One of the most important traditional arts in Japan is the *sadou,* or tea ceremony. Tourists should not pass the opportunity to take some lessons on this, especially since drinking *matcha* (thick green tea) is becoming a trend in the Western society.

Clothing in modern Japan now leans more toward the Western style. However, on special occasions, the locals would still put on their traditional costumes. The most popularly-known one is the *kimono*, which is made of silk, cotton, or wool. Men wear black kimono, while women wear colorful ones. The sash that envelopes the waist is called the *obi*. Travelers who are passionate about Japanese style and culture can purchase kimono from a store, but much of those in Tokyo are extremely expensive. More affordable ones can be found in Kyoto during sales.

One cannot talk about Japanese culture without mentioning martial arts. Although this topic would call for an entire book on its own, one should just remember that there are two types of Japanese martial arts: the ones that end in -*dou* and the ones that end in -*jitsu*. -*dou* refers to the martial arts that train one to do a *certain 'way' of being* (such as *judou*), while the -*jitsu* refers to a martial art that is designed for combat (such as *jujitsu*).

Sumou is the classic wrestling sport in Japan and is influenced by Shintou religion. A sumou tournament is called *basho* and starts and ends on Sunday, a period that lasts for 15 days. Those who wish to witness this should choose to visit Japan in any of the following months: January, May and September (in Tokyo), March (in Osaka), July (in Nagoya), and November (in Fukuoka).

Religion

In Japan, their native religion is Shintou, which is the belief that spirits are ever-present in all natural things. It cannot really be described as a complex religion, but rather a more ritualistic in the sense that practitioners would engage in prayer and rituals to receive good luck from the gods. This is why older Japanese, and some young ones, would always turn to a shrine upon passing it and then bow their heads to the spirits that dwell within.

In the 6th century, Mahayana Buddhism entered and flourished in Japan. Practitioners then began dividing into sects for the next several hundred years.

Nowadays, many Japanese would refer to themselves as atheist, and do not really understand the concept of taking on strong moral stands. Most Japanese in the modern-day society are in fact content with enjoying life and finding pleasure in hard work.

Chapter 2: Japan Survival Guide for Travelers

There are loads of little details that you should know before going to Japan to enjoy the culture and scenery without feeling uncomfortable. This section is dedicated to just that.

Download Apps for Travelers

The first thing that you should do is to download all the mobile applications designed specifically for travelers to Japan into your phone, such as *Navitime for Japan Travel*, which will provide you with Japan's subway maps (including subways, local and express trains, and bullet trains), schedules and ticket prices.

Another great app is a Scanner and Translator app that will allow you to understand Japanese characters simply by taking a photo with your phone and then letting the app translate it to English. Amazing!

Instead of panicking your way through dictionary pages, there are several apps that use speech recognition technology to translate English to Japanese and vice versa. However, they only work effectively for simple phrases and conversations.

There are tons of other apps that you can download and use extensively throughout your trip. Try them out before you leave for Japan so that you can have them all nicely installed and set up by the time you get there.

Bring your own medicine and toiletries

Roll-on deodorants with antiperspirant and tampons are a rare commodity in Japan, so make sure to pack those if you think you need them. Japanese and Western medicines do not differ much, but of course, the labels are written in Japanese and it would be highly inconvenient to try and buy one during emergencies. Therefore, the solution is to simply pack your own medicine. In case you were not able to bring a certain type of medicine, you can walk to a nearby pharmacy, ask for a clerk or pharmacist who can speak in English, and ask for the meds needed.

On Arrival

One of the most daunting times that any first-time traveler might face upon arrival to a foreign destination is when they get out of the airport terminal. To help shake off the uneasy feeling, you can go to the nearest bathroom and then relieve yourself after that long plane ride. Then, head over to where you can change money. You can have your currency changed for a nominal fee in kiosks near the airport. Keep in mind that Japan has a cash-based shopping culture and that credit and debit cards are generally not accepted. The standard pocket money in Japan is 30,000 JPY or 300 USD.

Standard Customs

One of the worst things that could possibly happen to you while you are in Japan is to offend the locals. Of course, the Japanese are quite patient and understanding of foreigners, but it always helps to be polite. Here are some tips to help you avoid awkward social interactions.

First, learn how to say thank you, excuse me, and please in Japanese. Thank you is *"arigatou gozaimasu"*, excuse me is *"sumimasen"*, and please is *"o kudasai"*, which is often said after your request. This is especially useful when you are out shopping. Something to remember as well is that it is not customary to strike up a conversation with store clerks, unless they are foreigners themselves.

Keep in mind that tipping is considered rude in Japan. If you truly appreciate the help of the cab driver, store clerk, or waiter, a cheerful *"arigatou gozaimasu"* would be more appreciated.

In Japan, bowing is the equivalent of shaking someone's hand. You can practice bowing your head down or take it a step further for superiors by bowing at the waist. Also, it is important to address people by their titles (such as Doctor Koji) or by attaching -*san* at the end (such as Koji-sama). An even more respectful suffix is -*sama*. Unless you are close friends with a Japanese person of the same age, you should only call younger people, especially children, by their first names. You can also attach the suffix -*chan* to a little girl's name or -*kun* to a boy's if you want to practice using the language.

Here is a warning: never ever be late for any appointment. Even one minute of tardiness is considered incredibly rude. You will notice that everything is on the clock in Japanese society: even trains are never more than 30 seconds late.

On entering a home or even most hotels and business establishments, it is customary to take off one's shoes so as not to bring in outside dirt. Be sensitive of this by observing the behavior of those who enter the threshold of a building so you can follow suit. A shoe rack is always located close to the entrance. Also, a pair of slippers will either be provided for you or will just be nearby for you to slip into. If you want to carry your own slippers, you can easily find cheap foldable ones in a 100-yen shop nearby.

There will be times when you need to take off even your indoor slippers. One common case is when you have to step onto a *tatami* mat. Another one is when you have to enter a bathroom; leave your slippers outside and then put on the rubber slippers that are kept inside, worn solely in the bathroom.

Table Manners

You must have heard of all sorts of unusual dining customs in Japan. Well, most of them are probably true. For instance, it is true that you should let the chef hear you slurping up your bowl of ramen so as to let him know that you absolutely love it.

It is perfectly acceptable to raise the bowl up to your mouth so that you can guide the food into it more easily using your chopsticks. Speaking of which, it might be a good idea to start practicing on your chopstick wielding skills before you go to Japan.

When eating at a restaurant in Japan, you are most likely going to be hand a small, wet cloth. This is used to wiping your hands before you eat. After wiping, make sure to fold it neatly and then place it on the table. Never use it as a napkin.

Right before you eat, it is advised that you say *itidakimasu,* which translates to *"I will receive".* It is the Japanese counterpart to the *bon appetit* of the French.

Public Bathhouse Manners

The tradition of bathing in a *sento* (public bathhouse) lives on in Japan. You can find them in most, if not all, major cities and small towns. While most popular *sento* will provide foreigners with a guide on how to use the facilities, it is nevertheless important to know your way around beforehand.

The Japanese bath is used only after you have thoroughly washed the body and rinsed off all dirt and grime. Once you are all squeaky clean, you can then step into the super-hot water of the *ofuro* (Japanese tub) for up to 30 minutes.

Overall Safety

Japan in general has low crime rate. In fact, in 2014, it was revealed that Japan is *the safest country in the world* according to a study by the Organization of Economic Cooperation and Development. However, that does not mean you should no longer exercise safety measures at all times, especially if your physical features are significantly different. Women in particular should take great care. As Japan is a predominantly old-fashioned society as far as gender is concerned, men are therefore still perceived as holding the higher power over the opposite sex.

To avoid attracting predators and stalkers, walk purposefully and with confidence as if you know your way around (even if you don't all the time). You should also avoid walking alone at night in not-so-populated areas such as dark streets. Make sure to lock your door at all times, and to never accept invitations into a home of a person you barely know. Most of all, update your loved ones on how you are doing and where you are located. You know, just in case.

Chapter 3: Tokyo

Tokyo is the capital city of Japan. It is a major international finance center, which means that it's quite a busy place to be in. In spite of that, it still attracts plenty of tourists because it offers a wide variety of attractions, often a mixture of the traditional and the modern. Choose from among its wide selections of museums, theaters for performing arts, and cuisine.

Tokyo also happens to be the world's most populated metropolis, so it is easy to say that you should expect a lot of people there. This 2016, Tokyo's "10 Year Project for Green Tokyo" will come into fruition, and its aim is to grow and maintain a million roadside trees, so you should expect just as many trees as there are skyscrapers. The urban landscape of Tokyo is consisting primarily of modern architecture, so do not feel disappointed when you do not see any traditional-looking buildings there. However, lurking within those massive giants of steel and concrete, there are plenty of traditional shops that offer unique and authentic experiences.

Best Times to Visit

The ideal time for tourists to go to Tokyo is between the months of September and November, because the fall temperature is cool and the surroundings are a beautiful golden orange. This is a great time to go to the parks and visit all the best spots, just remember to bring a light jacket with you and wear it, especially during nighttime. October is the Tokyo International Film Festival, so be there if you are fond of watching Japanese and other foreign films. Three main events take place in November: 3 is Culture Day, 15 is Seven-Five-Three Festival, and 23 is Labor Thanksgiving Day.

Winter between December and February might be a good idea if you want to avoid the crowds, but there is a reason why there are not a lot of people: it can get freezing cold. As for key events, the Japanese celebrate the Emperor's birthday on December 23, New Year's Day on January 1, and National Foundation Day on February 11.

Springtime is a glorious season in Tokyo because the whole megalopolis is filled with the world renowned Japanese cherry blossoms, especially between March and April. There will be large crowds during this time, so be prepared for that. Anime and art enthusiasts should schedule their travel around this time as in these months the Tokyo International Anime Fair and the Art Fair Tokyo are held. The Japanese Golden Week, which is a series of public holidays starts on April 29 and ends on May 5.

You can also choose to visit during summertime, which happens to be the peak tourist season. But be prepared for long queues, immense heat, and having to fight for reservations. Nevertheless, if you are serious about attending the Fuji Rock Festival in July or the Asakusa Samba Festival in August, or witnessing the Sumida River Fireworks on the last Saturday of July, then all is worth it.

Where to Go and What to See

Tokyo's Top Sights

Meiji Jingu Shrine

As the name suggests, this shrine is dedicated to Emperor Meiji and Empress Shoken. It is one of the most popular shrines in Japan. Many traditional Shinto weddings are held here throughout the year. Since it is surrounded by a large forested area, entering the shrine grounds through the massive *torri* gate instantly replaces the sounds of a bustling city with an air of quiet tranquility.

Activities include making offerings, buying amulets and charms and writing a wish on an *ema*. You can also find the Meiji Jingu Treasure House and an inner garden.

Hours:

Shrine: sunrise to sunset

Treasure House and Inner Garden: 9AM to 4:30AM

Admission Fee:

Shrine: Free

Treasure House and Inner Garden: ¥500

How to Get Here:

Take the JR Yamanote Line to Harajuku Station.

Tsukiji Fish Market

This is Tokyo's most famous wholesale market for fish, meat and other fresh produce, especially its tuna auction. However, the market's infrastructure was not designed to host a large amount of people, thus, being a major tourist spot has become a problem for many vendors. Visitors are encouraged to see the outer market, instead. Here, you'll find various restaurants and small retail shops. You can have a fresh sushi breakfast at one of the restaurants.

Hours:

Outer Market: 5AM to 2PM

Inner Market: 9AM until end of visitation

Closed:

Sundays and national holidays

How to Get Here:

From Tokyo Station, take the Marunouchi Subway line to Ginza, then transfer to Hibiya Subway line to Tsukiji Station.

From Shinjuku, take the Oedo Subway line to Tsukiji Shijo Station.

Tokyo Tower

Located at the heart of Tokyo, the Tokyo Tower was Japan's answer to Paris' Eiffel Tower back in 1958. It symbolized Japan's rebirth as a major economic superpower. Today, it remains the tallest self-supported steel tower of the world. It is used for broadcasting Japanese media signals.

Below the tower stands a four-story building called FootTown. It houses various museums, cafes, restaurants, souvenir shops and the One Piece Tower amusement park. The amusement park offers a selection of games, shows and other forms of entertainment that feature the characters from the popular manga. The museums, found in the third and fourth floors, include the Guinness World Records Museum and the Tokyo Tower Wax Museum.

Hours:

Observatories: 9AM to 11PM

One Piece Tower: 10AM to 10PM

Admission Fees:

Main Observatory: ¥900

Special Observatory charges an additional ¥600

One Piece Tower: ¥3200

Guinness World Records Museum: ¥700

The Wax Museum: ¥870

How to Get Here:

Five minutes' walk from the Onarimon, Akabanebashi, and Kamiyacho Stations.

Tokyo Skytree

This new television broadcasting tower has become the centerpiece of Sumida Ward. It is currently the tallest building in Japan and the second tallest in the world. The highlight of the Skytree is the two observation decks: Tembo Deck, the lower part, and Tembo Gallery, which is considered the highest skywalk in the world. These observation decks offer a spectacular 360-degree panoramic view of Tokyo at the heights of 350m and 450m respectively. In the Tembo Deck, you will find a souvenir shop, a French-Japanese restaurant and a café.

Hours:

8AM to 10PM

Closed:

No closing days

Admission Fee:

First observatory: ¥2060

Upper observatory: additional ¥1030

Imperial Palace and Imperial Palace East Gardens

The Imperial Palace has been the residence of the Imperial Family since 1868. It was the site of the former Edo Castle that used to house the Tokugawa shogun, who was the ruler of Japan from 1603 to 1867. When the shogunate was overthrown, the capital moved from Kyoto to Tokyo. The construction of the new palace was completed in 1888, but was later destroyed during World War II. After the war, it was later rebuilt in the same style.

After the tour, visitors can choose to enter the Imperial East Gardens via a private gate, letting them bypass the queue at the main entrance. The East Gardens are open to the general public. Most visitors use the Ote-mon gate. The best time to visit is during March and April since these are the plum and cherry blossom seasons.

Visitors are limited, so if you want to visit, you need to make reservations through their website:

Website: sankan.kunaicho.go.jp/order/index_EN.html

Hours:

Imperial Palace: 9AM to 5PM

Imperial Palace East Gardens: 9AM to 4:30PM

Closed:

Mondays, Fridays, New Year holidays

Admission Fee:

Free

How to Get Here:

From Narita, take the JR Narita Express Line to Tokyo Station.

Mount Takao (*Takaosan*)

Not all destinations in Tokyo are manmade. Takaosan, considered a sacred mountain, offers various hiking opportunities and a beautiful scenery. You can choose from a network of hiking trails that go up the slopes of Takaosan. Trail number 1 is the usual choice of visitors, since it is broader and more paved compared to the other trails. Trail 1 usually takes 90 minutes to reach the top, but you can use the cable car or car lift, which cuts halfway up the mountain, to save more time.

There are semi-limited express trains from Keio Shinjuku Station that directly connect to Takaosanguchi Station, which is located at the foot of the mountain. The ride takes about 50 minutes and costs ¥390.

Other than the hiking trails, a trip to Mount Takao offers these other attractions:

- **Yakuoin Temple** can be found along the trail near the summit. Tourist and locals alike stop there to pray to mountain gods or *tengu* for good fortune. Admission is free.

- **Monkey Park**, found at trail number 1, features a glass-walled enclosure, which is home to 40 Japanese macaques and a wild flower garden with over 500 types of plants. The park opens daily from 9:30AM to 4PM from December to February, 10AM to 4:30PM from March to April, and 9:30AM to 4:30PM from May to November. Admission fee is ¥420.

- **Keio Takaosan Onsen Gokurakuyu**, found at the base of the mountain. It is a hot spring bath house with gender segregated baths. Operating hours starts from 8AM to 11PM every day. Admission fee is ¥1000 on regular days and ¥1200 during autumn and New Year holidays.

The cable cars and car lifts are also considered an attraction. Cable cars operate daily from 8AM to 5:45PM and depart every 15 minutes. One way rides cost ¥480, while round trips cost around ¥930. On the other hand, the car lifts operate from 9AM to 4:30PM (until 4PM from December to April) every day. Fees are similar.

Odaiba

Odaiba is one of the most popular entertainment and shopping destinations in Tokyo, set in a large manmade island, which features unique, sometimes strange, hypermodern buildings.

Here are some of its popular points of interest:

- The **Fuji TV Building**, headquarters of Fuji Television, is one of Odaiba's notable landmarks. The building looks like it was made out of tinker toys. Entrance to the building is free, but access to its futuristic-looking, sphere-shaped observatory desk comes with a price.

  Hours:

  10AM to 6PM

Mondays

Admission Fee:

¥550

- The **Oedo Onsen Monogatari** is Tokyo's largest hot spring complex. Fashioned into Edo-era style, it features an almost endless array of indoor and outdoor baths fed by natural underground water pumped from a 1400m depth. You can also find plenty of souvenir shops, bar and restaurants. Massages and overnight stays are available, too.

Hours:

11AM to 9AM

Closed:

No closing days

Admission Fee:

¥2480 (drops to ¥1980 after 6PM but charges an additional ¥2000 overnight fee after 2AM)

- Tokyo **Leisureland** is a huge entertainment complex, which features various arcades, slot machines, bowling alleys, batting cages, darts, karaoke, table tennis and other sports games. It also has a haunted house, a ninja illusion house and a food court.

Hours:

10AM to 11:50PM (some parts open for 24hrs)

Closed:

No closing days

Admission Fee:

Free (each attraction charges differently)

- The **Tokyo Big Sight** is Japan's biggest exhibition and convention center. It has one of the boldest architectural designs in Odaiba. Various events are held here, including the Comiket Comic Fair, Tokyo Motor Show, Tokyo International Anime Fair, etc. The price of the admission depends on the event.

- The two-story **Rainbow Bridge** connects Odaiba to the main land. It is one of the most beautiful bridges in Japan, decorated with hundreds of lights that change according to seasons. You can appreciate it better during the night when it is brightly illuminated.

- The **Giant Gundam Robot** displayed in front Divers City Tokyo Plaza is also a popular attraction. Fans of the anime series should not miss the opportunity to see the life-size replica of RX-78-2 Gundam.

How to Get Here:

Take the Yurikamome train to Shimbashi Station. Unfortunately, the Yurikamome is not included in the JR Pass. One ride may cost about ¥320, so if you plan to ride it more than twice, get a 1-day pass for ¥820 instead.

Take the Tokyo Water Bus from Hinode Pier to Odaiba. Travel takes 20 minutes and costs ¥480.

Cross the Rainbow Bridge on foot (bicycles are not allowed). Note that the pedestrian walkway is closed from 9PM to 9AM (6PM to 10AM from November to March) daily. It also closes every third Monday of the month, from December 29 to 31, and during the fireworks display in Tokyo Bay.

Edo-Tokyo Museum

Considered as one of the best museums in Tokyo, the Edo-Tokyo Museum features the history of the metropolis from 1590, when it was designated as the new capital of the nation, up to the fire bombings in World War II. The uncanny design of the building is as interesting as its collections. Inside, you can find life-size replicas of buildings such as the Nakamuraza Theater and the Choya Newspaper Publishing Co. of the old Ginza. Visitors will learn much about the Edo Period - their way of life, political climate, architecture, etc. - in an interactive way.

Hours:

9:30AM to 5:30AM (until 7:30PM on Saturdays)

Closed

Mondays and New Year holidays

Admission Fee

¥600 (additional fees apply for special exhibitions)

Tokyo Dome City

Tokyo Dome City is an entertainment complex, which features the following attractions:

- The **Tokyo Dome**, nicknamed Big Egg, is the biggest roofed baseball stadium of the world. It can seat 55,000 people. The stadium is not exclusive to games. Festivals, concerts and other events are also held here. Operating hours and admission fees vary depending on the event.

- The **Tokyo Dome City Attractions** is an amusement park, which features a number of extreme rides and various entertainment facilities. Operations start at 10AM to 9PM every day. Admission fee is ¥3900.

- The **Korakuen Hall** is an arena famous for hosting boxing, mix-martial arts, and professional wrestling matches. Operating hours and admission fees vary depending on the event.

You can access Tokyo Dome City from Suidobashi Station via JR Chuo Line or from Korakuen Station via Marunouchi or Namboku Subway Lines or from Kasuga Station via Oeda or Mita Subway Lines.

Ghibli Museum

Studio Ghibli is one of the most famous animation studios in Japan, known for its award-winning animation films such as Spirited Away, Princess Mononoke, and My Neighbor Totoro. The Ghibli Museum features many characters and articles from the films, including a life-sized statues of Totoro and the robot from the film "Castle in the Sky." The structure itself has a whimsical and almost cartoonish design. You will also find a café, rooftop garden, play area for kids and a souvenir shop.

Hours:

10AM to 6PM

Closed:

Tuesday and New Year holidays

Admission Fee:

¥1000

How to Get Here:

Located in Mikata, you can easily reach the museum via the JR Chuo Line to Mikata Station. From the station, you can either take the shuttle bus (¥210) or taxi (¥750) to the museum. You can also walk, which only takes about 20 minutes.

Tokyo Disneyland

Disneyland is a popular theme park based on various Disney films. Tokyo Disneyland is the first Disney theme park outside the US. It offers seven themed lands -Adventureland, Fantasyland, Critter Country, World Bazaar, Toontown, Tomorrowland, and Westernland.

Hours:

9AM to 10PM (opens 8AM on weekends and holidays)

Closed:

No closing days

Admission Fee:

¥6900

How to Get Here:

Take the JR Keiyo or Musashino line to Maihama Station or take the Disney Resort Monorail to Tokyo Disneyland Station.

Tokyo DisneySea

This fantasy theme park is unique to Japan. Similar to Disneyland, DisneySea also features seven themed areas, but instead of lands, it has ports of call. These are the Mediterranean Harbor, Mermaid Lagoon, Mysterious Island, Arabian Coast, Port Discovery, Lost River Delta and American Waterfront. It was inspired by sea myths and legends. Though it is open to all ages, this theme park was probably designed to be more appealing to the grown-ups as it has wider food selection and alcoholic beverages.

DisneySea is located next to Tokyo Disneyland. You can take the Disney Resort Monorail to the Tokyo DisneySea Station or you can walk from Maihama Station, which takes about 20 minutes.

Fees and operation hours are similar to that of Tokyo Disneyland.

Kabukiza Theater

Located at Ginza, Chuo-ku, this theater is arguably the best place to see *kabuki*. It features various plays almost every day. Regular tickets for entire plays usually cost between ¥4000 and ¥22000 and require advance reservations, while single acts cost ¥2000. You can buy them on the same day at the theater. +81 (0)3-3545-6800

How to Get Here:

Take the Marunouchi, Hibiya, or Ginza Line and connect to Ginza Station. It is also a few minutes' walk from the JR Yurakucho or Shimbashi Stations.

Ryogoku Kokugikan

This is Japan's largest sumo arena, which can hold more than 10,000 viewers. *Basho* or grand tournaments are held every January, May, and September. The second floor Western-style chairs start from ¥3600 to ¥8400, while the first floor Japanese-style box seats cost ¥9200, ¥10300, and ¥11300. You can purchase the tickets a month before the tournament. Another option is to buy unsold seats on the same day of the match for only ¥2100.

Asakusa District

This was once Tokyo's largest red light district complete with geisha, courtesans, actors, gangsters and even beggars. However, the entire area was destroyed during World War II. When it was reconstructed, the pleasure districts were diminished. Until now, majority of its area were preserved, and most of them date back to the postwar reconstructions in the 1950s.

Points of interest:

- Sensoji Temple is considered as Tokyo's most famous Buddhist temple. Built in the 7th century, Senso-ji is one of the oldest temples in the world. Admission is free. It opens from 6AM to 5PM.

- Nakamise Shopping Street, located near the temple, caters to the temple's visitors. It is lined with over 50 shops where you can buy local specialties, traditional snacks and souvenirs.

You can easily explore Asakusa on foot, but you can also try a guided tour on *rickshaw*. The tour takes about 30 minutes and costs around ¥9000 for two people.

Ueno District

To feel the old Tokyo vibe, a visit to Ueno is a must. Unlike Asakusa, which has recently constructed a few modern buildings, Ueno is entirely without high-rise condos or modern shopping centers. The good thing about it being completely "downtown" is that the prices are significantly cheaper. However, take extra caution around the southwest area of Ueno Station, which is a red light district.

The main attraction here is the Ueno Park, which is surrounded by numerous Buddhist temples and several museums, including the Tokyo National Museum - the oldest and largest museum in Japan. It is made of several buildings that house many important cultural artifacts and national treasures. Museum hours start from 9:30AM to 5PM every day, except Mondays. Admission fee is ¥620.

Best Gardens and Parks

Rikugi-en

Considered as Tokyo's most beautifully landscaped garden, features a large central pond, landscaped hills, forested areas, open lawns, all connected by several winding paths. It also has several teahouses that offer tea for ¥510. The garden is based on the 16th century waka poetry.

Hours:

9AM to 5PM

Admission Fee:

¥300

How to Get Here:

Take the Namboku Subway Line or JR Yamanote Line to Komagome Station.

Hama-rikyu Gardens

Originally built for the shoguns, this 17th-century garden is now open to the public. It boasts an all-season array of flowers and flowering trees and a picturesque tea house set in the middle of the pond. Visitors can order green tea and sweets for ¥500.

Hours:

9AM to 5PM

Admission Fees:

¥300 for adults, ¥150 for seniors, free for primary school children

How to Get Here:

Seven minutes' walk from the Yurikamome Line and ten minutes' walk from the JR Shimbashi Station.

Shinjuku Gyoen National Garden

Originally designed as a private garden of the Imperial Family, the Shinjuku Gyoen is one of the best places for cherry blossom viewing in spring. In 1949, the garden was finally opened to the public. It offers an array of beautiful gardens, from Japanese and English to French layouts. It also has a Taiwanese teahouse and a botanical conservatory.

Hours:

9AM to 4:30PM

Closed:

Mondays and from December 29 to January 3

Admission Fees

¥200 for adults, ¥50 for children under 15, free for children under 6.

How to Get Here:

Ten minutes' walk from JR Shinjuku Station.

Yoyogi Park

One of the largest city parks in Tokyo, Yoyogi Park is famous for its ginko tree forest. While other parks are crowded in spring for cherry blossom viewing, this park is frequented during autumn for its remarkable golden brown ginko trees. It offers wide lawns, large ponds and a number of forested areas where you can have a picnic, jog, or do any other outdoor activities.

The park is always open with free admission. It is a 5-minute walk from Harajuku Station via the JR Yamanote Line.

Where and What to Eat

Must-Try: Sushi, Soba, Dojo-Nabe, Chanko-Nabe, Monja-Yaki

Budget

- Afuri

Look for this ramen bar in Ebisu at the back part of Ebisu Yokocho shopping center. If you are looking for some adventure, try their yuzu-scented yuzushio-men, or their golden soup with pork.

- Inaba Wako, Takashimaya (Shinjuku)

Tonkatsu, the deep fried, panko coated pork dish loved by everyone around the world, is the specialty of this place.

- Butayaro

Situated outside Ochanomizu Station, this eatery serves beer with their specialty *butadon,* which is pork on top of grilled rice.

- Momose

This is a tiny shop that is so popular you have to line up to get in. Their specialty is tempura, so do not forget to order that. Try their *anago baraage-don,* which is a crisp salt water eel tempura.

- Tsujita

This popular ramen shop serves a special kind of ramen called *tsukemen.* It has thick noodles and is served with lime and bits of pork.

- Ganso Zushi

Who can forget sushi? Enjoy budget-friendly tasty sushi in this shop, which serves them classic conveyor belt style.

- Sushi-Ro

Locals on a budget, such as college students, love to get some cheap yet delicious sushi from this place. Take your pick from the screen or by taking them from the conveyor belt. Each plate with two pieces of nigiri sushi is about 100 yen or more (not including tax).

High End

- Sawada (MC Building, 3F, 5-1-19 Ginza Chuo-kuo)

This fine dining restaurant has two Michelin stars under its belt and offers the promise of serving only the freshest wild fish in your sushi.

- Yukimura (Takayanagi Building 3F, 1-5-5 Azubu-juban, Minato)

The specialty of this place is creative Kyoto-style cuisine, with ingredients brought in from Kyoto.

- Sushi Kanesaka (8-10-3 Ginza)

Artist Takashi Murakami loves this edomae-style sushi restaurant so much. It also happens to have two Michelin stars.

- Tsujitome (1-8-5 Moto-Aksaka, Minoto-ku)

This exclusive restaurant serves kaiseki, a style of traditional Japanese cuisine where intricate dishes are served.

- Hamadaya (Nihonbashi Ningyo-cho, 3-13-5 Ningyo-cho, Nihonbashi, Chuo-ku)

This high end traditional Japanese restaurant offers the services of geisha to host celebrations.

Where to Stay

Low Budget

- Khaosan Tokyo Guest House Ninja (2-5-1 Nihombashi Bakurocho, Chuo-ku)

Contact number: +81 3 6905 9205

This inexpensive hotel offers dormitory-type rooms, which may not be a good choice for couples but a perfect one for backpackers and solo travelers on a budget. Social people will enjoy their stay here because the hotel throws small parties for guests.

- Ryokan Sansuiso (2-9-5 Higashi Gotanda, Shinagawa-ku, Gotanda)

Contact number: +81 3 3441 7475

This budget-friendly hotel is close to popular destination sites. You get to sleep on futon beds and experience the traditional Japanese shared bath. However, it might not be a good place to stay in if you plan to be out past midnight because that is their curfew.

- Tokyu Stay Shibuya (8-14 Shinsencho, Shibuya-ku)

Contact number: +81 3 3477 1091

This budget hotel is designed specifically for those who are in Tokyo for business, but who do not plan on splurging. Its rooms have kitchenettes as well as laundry facilities.

- Ryokan Katsutaro (4-16-8 Ikenohata, Taito-ku)

Contact number: +81 3 3828 2500

If you plan on going shopping at Ginza or visit museums and art galleries, then you should consider staying in this budget-friendly hotel. You can even rent bicycles for those who wish to get lost along the bike trails of Tokyo.

- Sakura Hotel Jimbocho (2-21-4 Kanda-Jimbocho, Chiyoda-ku)

Contact number: +81 3 3261 3939

If one of your main goals for visiting Tokyo is to check out the Imperial Palace, then you might want to consider checking into this hotel. It has dormitory rooms designed for those who plan to go out on a little adventure.

Mid-range Budget

- Hotel Century Southern Tower (2-2-1 Yoyogi, Shibuya-ku)

Contact number: +81 3 5354 0111

On top of the Shinjuku skyscraper you will find this fresh and modern hotel. It is conveniently close to the Shinjuku Station, making it the perfect place for travelers.

- Tokyu Stay Aoyama Premier (2-27-18 Minami-Aoyama, Minato-ku)

Contact number: +81 3 3497 0109

This affordable place offers rooms with built-in laundry and kitchen facilities, enabling travelers on a budget to enjoy their long-term stay without burning a hole in their pockets.

- Hilltop Hotel (1-1 Surugadai, Kanda)

Contact number: +81 3 3293 2311

For a more historic feel, you should stay in this hotel, which has been standing since 1937. Enjoy its Art Deco theme and charming vintage details.

- Hotel Gracery (7-10-1 Ginza, Chuo-ku)

Contact number: +81 3 6686 1000

Where else can you find a more thoughtful hotel for the ladies than this one? This hotel offers a floor just for women, with each room cleverly decorated and prepared to perfection.

High End

- Mandarin Oriental (2-1-1 Nihombashi Marumachi, Chuo-ku)

Contact Number: +81 3 3270 8800

This hotel can be found on the opposite side of Mitsukoshi department store and has huge rooms with amazing views to offer, together with five-star restaurants and glamorous entertainment centers.

- The Peninsula Tokyo (1-8-1 Yurakucho, Chiyoda-ku)

Contact number: +81 3 6270 2888

This hotel is close to Hibiya, Ginza, and Marunouchi, and is perfect for both business travelers and tourists who prefer to relax in a low-key place of luxury. One of the perks it offers to guests is a free drive to any place within 1-kilometer radius, in a Rolls Royce.

- Four Seasons Hotel Tokyo, Chinzan-So (2-10-8 Sekiguchi, Bunkyo-ku)

Contact Number: +81 3 5222 7222

Located in northeast Tokyo, this hotel has an ambiance that is fusion of Asian and European themes. It also has one of the most popular spas in Tokyo and boasts of spectacular garden views.

- The Ritz-Carlton Tokyo (9-7-1 Akasaka, Minato-ku)

Contact Number: +81 3 3423 8000

This hotel is touted to be one of the best in Japan and is found in the tallest building in Tokyo. It is also the perfect place to stay in for couples who are more than ready to splurge.

- Park Hyatt Tokyo (3-7-1-2 Nishi-Shinjuku, Shinkuku-ku)

Contact Number: +81 3 5322 1234

If you have seen the movie *Lost in Translation,* you would definitely be familiar with this glamorous hotel and its sunlit indoor swimming pool on the 47th floor.

Nightlife

Roppongi District

Roppongi is Tokyo's most popular nightlife district among foreigners. It offers numerous restaurants, bars and nightclubs that cater specifically to foreigners or are at least foreigner-friendly. Because of that, the district has the most diverse population in the city. It also houses several embassies.

Other than its nightlife, the district has recently gained a reputation as an arts center due to the construction of the National Art Center, Mori Art Museum and Suntory Museum of Art. These museums form the "Art Triangle Roppongi."

How to Get Here:

From Tokyo Station, take the Hibiya or Marunouchi Subway lines via the Kasumigaseki Station.

From Shinjuku, take the Oedo Subway line to Roppongi Station.

Kabukicho

Japan's largest red light district offers numerous nightclubs, restaurants, pachinko parlors, bars and love hotels. Remember to take caution when exploring this area. There were some incidences that resulted to loss of credit cards and cash due to drunkenness.

Hours:

Restaurants: 11AM to 12AM (some shops open for 24hrs)

Bars: 7PM until morning

Closed:

Some close on Sundays

Omoide Yokocho

Nicknamed as Piss Alley, this narrow network of alleyways is full of dozens of tiny drinking establishments and eateries that serve ramen, sushi, soba, kushiyaki, and yakitori. Most of them consist of only one counter and several chairs lined in front. Here, you will get the feel of an authentic Japanese pub scene.

Hours:

5PM to 12AM (some shops open for lunch)

Japanese Pubs

- Bar Ishiohana, located near the Shibuya Station, is high-end bar, which offers artful drinks. Open all days from 6PM-2AM. ☎ 81 03-5485-8405

- Tengu, located in an alley between Inokashira-dori and Center Gai, is a popular Japanese pub, which has English menu. Opens from 5PM until midnight.

- Hatago, located along Dogenzaka Street, is a stylish Japanese pub, which also accommodates foreign customers. A meal including drinks can cost about ¥3000 per person.

- Happy Dining Ghetto, located at the 3rd floor Center Building, serves an extensive food and drink selection and generally caters to the young Shibuya crowd.

- The Lock Up, located at Center-gai, is a themed *izakaya* with a long hallway that is more like a haunted house than an entrance. It has a dungeon themed eatery, which features food with brutal names, test tube cocktails, handcuffs, prison breaks, etc. Meals range from ¥400-820 and draft beer cost about ¥500. ☎ +81 03-5728-7731

Bars and Night Clubs

- Manpuku Shokudo, located directly under the tracks of Yurakucho Station, is a traditional Japanese *izakaya* (drinking establishment), which offers draft beers and sake along with typical Japanese comfort foods. It is open for 24 hours and costs around ¥300. ☎ 81-3-3221-6001.

- Peter: The Bar offers a wide selection of luxurious vintage concoctions. It is located at 24th floor of The Peninsula Hotel.

- Club Air, located at B2 Hikawa Bldg., was featured in the movie *Lost in Translation*. ☎ +81 03-6145-6231

- Harlem, located in Tuburayama-cho, is a two-floor hip-hop club. Foreigners will only be admitted if they are accompanied by a Japanese friend. ☎ +81 03-3461-8806

- Popeye Beer Club in Ryogoku is probably the best place in Tokyo to try Japanese microbrews. It also has interesting food selections with English menus. Pints of beer cost around ¥900. ☎ +81 03-3633-2120

Chapter 4: Kyoto

For over a thousand years, Kyoto was the formal Imperial capital of Japan, hence it is referred to as the *thousand-year capital*. Those who wish to experience a predominantly traditional side of Japanese culture should visit this city, especially as 20 percent of the National Treasures of the country are there, as well as 17 UNESCO World Heritage Sites.

The festivals held in Kyoto have been celebrated for over a thousand years as well. During these times, tourists teem in to get a glimpse of, and somehow immerse themselves in, the ancient traditions of Japan. There are over 400 Shinto shrines and 1,600 Buddhist temples as well, so those who are on a spiritual pilgrimage must not miss out. Because of its utterly captivating and romantic scenery and architecture, Kyoto is the center for Japan's television and film industry. Movies of samurai, geisha, and the Imperial family in traditional settings are frequently shot there.

Best Times to Visit

Many seasoned travelers to Kyoto would agree that fall (October to November) and spring seasons (March to May) are the best times to enjoy Kyoto.

October is a great time to visit for history enthusiasts because the Festival of Ages is usually held on the on the 22dn. People dressed in period costumes would parade from the Kyoto Imperial Palace to Heian-jingu Shrine. But choose wisely, for on the same day, another festival is held in Kurama village, and it is when young men would carry flaming torches across the street dressing in loincloths.

Try to book your trip around mid-March to witness the bloom of plum blossoms at the Kyoto Gosho or the Kitano-Tenmangu Shrine. If you can only visit in April, then you can enjoy their cherry blossoms instead, at the Maruyama-koen Park or the Kyoto Botanical Gardens. May is said to be the most beautiful month because it is not only the peak of spring but also a month full of festivals. You can enjoy the Yabusame or horseback archery festival at the Shimogamo-jinja Shrine, and take part in the Aoi Matsuri festival.

However, if your trip happens to fall in another month, do not worry because the weather is mostly temperate year-round. Just be prepared to dress accordingly because the winter (December to February) can get quite cold.

On the 1st of January, you might be interested in taking part in the first shrine visit of the New Year festival called *Hatsumode*. Archery enthusiasts should witness the Toshiya Festival on January 15, which is held at the Sanjusangen-do Temple. From February 2 to 4, you can attend the Setsubun Matsuri fire festival at the Yoshida-jinja Shrine.

In summer (June to August), the weather can become humid. However, you can expect a few rains between June and July. On July 17, you can join in on the biggest festival of the year in Kyoto, the Gion Matsuri and witness the festival floats in downtown Kyoto. During August, you can enjoy the Daimon-ji Fire Festival.

Where to Go and What to See

Heian Jungu

Constructed in 1895 to mark the 1100th anniversary of Kyoto and in dedication to Emperors Kammu and Komei, Heian Jungu is well known for possessing the biggest torii within the entire country. One of the best times to visit this Shinto shrine is on the 22nd of October when the Festival of Ages, also known as Jidai Matsuri, takes place. This festival is to celebrate when Kyoto was made the capital of Japan and includes a fantastic procession that trails on for miles and features over two thousand participants.

Hours:

0600 – 1730 Heian Shrine

0830 – 1700 Heian Shrine Garden

Admission Fee:

Free Heian Shrine

600 yen Heian Shrine Garden

How to Get Here:

97 Okazaki Nishitennocho, Sakyo-ku, Kyoto 606-8341, Kyoto Prefecture. Catch the City bus #5 or 100 from Kyoto Station or take the subway to Higashiyama Station; from here it is a short ten-minute walk.

Gion

Geishas have long been an icon of Japanese culture. They are a living, breathing testament to history. The best place to see geisha and maiko is at Gion. This district dates back several centuries and due to being declared a national historical preservation district, it has been beautifully preserved, with many buildings and entertainment venues exactly as it was hundreds of years ago. As you walk along the streets, you may see beautiful young geisha stroll with you.

Please note: despite misconceptions, geisha are not prostitutes and Gion is not a red-light district.

Hours:

All day.

Admission Fee:

Free.

How to Get Here:

Gionmachi, Higashiyama-ku, Kyoto 605-0001, Kyoto Prefecture. Take the #100 or 206 bus from Kyoto Station to the Gion bus stop, which takes around 20 minutes. The nearest train stations are Gion Shijo Station and Kawaramachi Station.

Kinkakuji (Golden Pavilion Temple)

The Golden Pavilion Temple is undoubtedly Kyoto's number one attraction. It takes its name from the golden leaves that spread over the top two levels of the pavilion and creates a spectacular spectacle. Kinkakuji is situated adjacent to a pond and the reflection of the pavilion in its crystal clear waters have long been a popular photo shoot for visitors. It also symbolizes the relationship between the divine world and the earthly one. Inside, the temple holds a wealth of Buddhist relics and artifacts.

Hours:

0900 – 1700

Admission Fee:

400 yen

1 Kinkakujicho, Kita-ku, Kyoto 603-8361, Kyoto Prefecture. Take the #101 or 205 bus from Kyoto Station or else take the subway to Kitaoji Station and then a taxi or bus to the temple.

Ginkakuji (Silver Pavilion Temple)

Initially, the Silver Pavilion Temple was meant to be a smaller, silvery version to the beforementioned Golden Pavilion Temple, but Ginkakuji is much more than that. The pavilion boasts two levels, its façade a beautifully and richly minimalist work of art, which is then carried on within the walls. Outside, the temple sits within two gardens, which add to the serene atmosphere. The first garden includes a pond, rocks and a variety of flora. The second garden boasts two interesting sand mountains, creating a peaceful atmosphere to enjoy.

Hours:

0830 – 1700 March to November, 0900 – 1630 December to February

Admission Fee:

500 yen

How to Get Here:

2 Ginkakuji-cho Sakyo-ku, Kyoto 606-8402, Kyoto Prefecture. You can take the #5, 17 or 100 bus from Kyoto Station which takes around 40 minutes each way.

Kyoto Imperial Palace

Also known as the Kyoto Gosho, the Imperial Palace was the home of the Japanese royal family for centuries but was abandoned in 1868 when the capital was transferred to Tokyo. Over the centuries, the palace has been destroyed by fire several times and the building you see today dates back to 1855. The palace is surrounded by elongated walls, and consists of numerous gates, halls, buildings and gardens.

Hours:

9:00 to 17:00 (April to August)
9:00 to 16:30 (September and March)
9:00 to 16:00 (October to February)
Admission ends 40 minutes before closure.

Closed:

Mondays (or following day if Monday is a national holiday), 28th December to 4th January

Admission Fee:

Free

How to Get Here:

3 Kyoto-Gyoen Kamigyo-ku, Kyoto 602-0881, Kyoto Prefecture. Take a subway to Marutamachi or Imadegawa Station.

Kiyomizudera

Also known as the Pure Water Temple, Kiyomizudera certainly makes Japan's top ten must see attractions. It dates back to 780 by the Hosso, one of the earliest Buddhist sects to emerge in Japan. It is situated in the forested hills just to the outside of the city to the east, and was declared a UNESCO World Heritage Site. Head here to enjoy amazing views of Kyoto from the wooden terrace and explore over 1,200 years of history in one place. If you're not feeling well, head to the spring underneath the wooden terrace – the waters are said to contain healing properties and from which the temple takes its name.

Hours:

0600 – 1800

Admission Fee:

400 yen

How to Get Here:

1-294 Kiyomizu, Higashiyama-ku, Kyoto 605-0862, Kyoto Prefecture. Take bus #100 or 206 to Gojo-zaka or Kiyomizu-michi bus stops and then walk uphill for ten minutes.

Fushimi Inari

Fushimi Inari is a beautiful Shinto shrine dedicated to Inari, the Japanese god of rice who uses foxes to convey messages to and from him. Because of this, the shrine is richly decorated with statues of foxes. While you can stroll through the numerous tori gates any time of the day, try visiting at dusk – when the low lights are on, the sounds of nature and the wildlife in the area create a charming atmosphere.

Hours:

Always open

Admission Fee:

Free

How to Get Here:

Take the train to JR Inari Station, where the shrine is located just outside or it is a short walk away from the Fushimi Inari Station.

Tenryuji Temple

While Kyoto boasts a number of Buddhist and Shinto temples within its borders, Tenryuji Temple is certainly the most prominent Zen Temple. Meaning Heavenly Dragon Temple in Japanese, it was originally constructed as a villa for Emperor Go Daigo but after his demise, it was re-established as a temple in his honour.

A popular legend tells of how a Buddhist priest dreamed that a dragon arose from the river close to the site, which caused the priest to believe the spirit of the emperor was restless and that a temple should be constructed to calm him.

Over the centuries the temple has suffered eight fires, although the last was more than 150 years ago. Consequently, the building you see before you today is just over a century old, but the garden dates back to the 14th century.

Hours:

0830 – 1730 April to September

0830 – 1700 October to March

Admission Fee:

500 yen plus another 100 yen for admittance into the temple buildings

How to Get Here:

68 Saga Tenryuji Susukinobabacho, Ukyo-ku, Kyoto 616-8385, Kyoto Prefecture. Take the train to Keifuku Arashiyama Station or to JR Saga-Arashiyama Station, from where it is a short ten-minute walk away.

Ryoanji Temple

Ryoanji Temple means the Peaceful Dragon. This UNESCO World Heritage Site belongs to the Myoshinki School of the Rinzai branch of the Zen Buddhist sect. It is popular as the gardens showcase traditional culture in Japan, boasting raked sand, rocks and clay walls. If you're searching for Zen, then Ryoanji Temple is where you will find it.

Hours:

0800 to 1700 (March to November)
0830 to 1630 (December to February)

Admission Fee:

500 yen

How to Get Here:

Take the JR bus from Kyoto to the temple, which takes around 30 minutes, otherwise you can take the train to Ryoanji-michi Station from where it is a five to ten-minute walk away.

Nightlife

You will see a different side of Kyoto when the sun goes down. Most of the nightlife can be found between Sanjo-dori and Shijo-dori. For food, head to Pontocho, located just to the east of Kiyamachi, with restaurant after restaurant and bars with views over the Kamogawa River. On occasion, you may just see geisha and maiko stroll down the roads, their faces beautifully painted and hair piled up high.

In addition to the many restaurants and bars, Kyoto boasts a vibrant artistic and cultural scene which is only second to Tokyo.

Bars in Kyoto

A Bar

A Bar is a izakaya, or a traditional Japanese pub, with a restaurant. Enjoy a fun and relaxing atmosphere as you sample a range of delicious dishes and sip on a cold beer or two. Just be prepared to hunt for it as it is set back from the main area and is located up a few stairs.

Hours:

2000 – 0500

How to Get Here:

2/F Reiho Building, Nishi Kiyamachi, Kyoto, Japan. Telephone: (075) 213 2129.

Ace Café

Located on the 10th floor, Ace Café is famous for its outstanding views over the eastern hills. Try searching for any of the numerous shrines and temples as you dine on exquisite

Italian meals, sip on a glass of wine and enjoy friendly but attentive service.

How to Get Here:

All hours.

How to Get Here:

10 Floor Empire Building, Kiyamachi Sanjo agaru, Kyoto. Telephone: (075) 241 0009.

Ishimaru Shoten

Ishimaru Shoten is a popular bar but you may have trouble finding it. Situated in a tapered alley within Kiyamachi's nightlife area, you'll find it when you see the number 13 sign at the entrance of the alley. Enjoy a vibrant night out among locals and visitors without breaking the bank.

How to Get Here:

13 Roji (Alley), Kiyamachi Sanjo agaru, Kyoto. Telephone: (075) 213 0966.

Club Metro

Club Metro is one of the most popular places in Kyoto. Located by Jingu-Marutamachi Station, this underground club plays music of all genres and hosts both local and international DJs. Just make sure you have comfortable shoes on.

How to Get Here:

B1F Ebisu Building, Kawabata-Marutamachi, Saykyo-ku, Kyoto. Telephone: (075) 752 2787.

Club World

The largest club in Kyoto, Club world is the best place to visit if you want to have a good time. A massive place that sees DJs from all over the world play here, it also hosts a number of geisha and other local events.

How to Get Here:

97 Shinmachi Shijo-agaru Nishi-Kiyamachi, Kyoto. Telephone: (075) 213 4119.

Where and What to Eat

Must-Try: Yuba, Tofu, Kaiseki, Kyo-wagashi, Yudofu, Shojin ryori

Budget

- Kyoto Ramen Koji

This ramen restaurant offers cheap but delicious bowls in eight regional styles. Find it on the Kyoto Station building's 10th floor.

- Ganko

You will be surprised at how inexpensive yet satisfying the sushi is in this restaurant, which is close by the Sanjo-Ohashi Bridge.

- Warai

Cook your own affordable okonomiyaki, or savory hotcakes with different fillings, here.

- Yagura

Slurp up some nisshin soba (soba noodles with smoked herring) as well as other types of udon and soba in this place. It is found across the Minamiza kabuki theatre.

- Ootoya Teishoku

This restaurant can be found in the neighborhood called Sanjo-Kawaramachi, and it offers a variety of fish, pork, and chicken teishoku meal sets (teishoku is a meal set composed of miso soup, a vegetable side dish, a bowl of rice, and a meat or fish main dish).

High End

- Kitcho Arashiyama Honten (58 Susukinobaba-cho, Saga Tenryuji, Ukyo-ku)

Are you looking for the best and most lavish kaiseki in Kyoto? This is the place to go!

- Sushi-kappo Nakaichi (570-196 Gionmachi-minamigawa, Higashiyama-ku)

This place serves sushi in elegant surroundings and served in the quintessential Japanese style.

- Ramen Santouka (137 Daikoku-cho, Sanjo-sagaru higashi-gawa, Yamatooji-dori, Higashiyama-ku)

Looking for the absolute best ramen in Kyoto? This one comes highly recommended!

- Sumibi-kushiyaki Torito (1F Kamihara Building, 9-5 Higashimaruta-cho, Kawabata-higashi-iru, Marutamachi-dori, Sakyo-ku)

Enjoy their high end yakitori in style sans the tear-jerking smoke.

- Honke Owariya – Downtown Kyoto

Delve into the true atmosphere of downtown Kyoto in this restaurant that serves quite possibly the best soba. You will most likely be sitting on tatami mats, though, so this place is not for those with weak knees.

Where to Stay

Low Budget

- Hotel Unizo (Sanjosagaru, Kawaramachidori, Nakagyo-ku)

Contact number: +81 75 241 4125

Do not be surprised by the small size of these rooms, because this hotel offers comfort and excellent hospitality in a great location.

- Hotel Alpha (Sanjo-agaru-nisigawa, Kawaramachidori, Nakagyo-ku)

Contact number: +81 75 241 2000

This great budget hotel is a stone's throw away from Gion and offers small but clean rooms at cheap prices.

- Capsule Ryokan (204 Tsuchihashicho, Shichijo-dori, Aburano-koji, Shimogyo-ku)

Contact number: +81 75 344 1510

A short walk away from Kyoto Station, this interesting hotel offers the quirky Japanese *sleep in a capsule* and traditional Japanese inn (called *ryokan*) experience.

- 9hours capsule hotel (Termachi Dori Shijo-sagaru, Shimogyo-ku)

Contact number: +81 75 353 9005

Are you looking for a true blue budget hotel while staying in Kyoto? Check into this one. You will also enjoy the artsy vibe created by industrial designer Fumie Shibata and graphic designer Masaaki Hiromura.

Mid-range Budget

- Hotel Citadines Kyoto Karasuma Gojo (432 Matsuya-cho, Gojo-dori, Karasuma Higashi iru, Shimogyo-ku)

Contact number: +81 75 352 8900

This moderately-priced hotel is located in Central Kyoto and is perfect for couples and small groups. You can rent a bicycle and head off to downtown within minutes from this hotel.

- Dormy Inn Premium Kyoto Ekimae (558-8 Higashishiokoji-cho, Shimogyo-ku)

Contact number: +81 75 371 5489

If you are looking for a hotel that is not too pricey and is close to the Kyoto Station, then this one is your best bet. It is ideal for business travelers and has a charming classic appeal.

- Mitsui Garden Hotel Kyoto Shijo (707-1 Myodenji-cho, Shijo-sagaru, Nishinotoin-dori, Shimogyo-ku)

Contact number: +81 75 256 3331

This classy, reasonably priced business hotel enables its guests quick access to the train station, subway, and the shopping district of Shijo-dori.

- Best Western Hotel (457 Matsugae-cho, Kawaramachi-dori, Rokkaku nishi iru, Nakagyo-ku)

Contact number: +81 75 254 4055

This is for those of you who wish to stay in a hotel within the heart of Kyoto. It is worth mentioning as well that the Shinkyokoku Shopping Arcade and the Kawaramachi-dori are a few minutes' walk away from it.

High End

- The Ritz-Carlton, Kyoto (Kamogawa Nijo-Ohashi Hotori, Hokodencho, Nakagyp Ward)

Contact number: +81 75 546 555

This 5-start hotel offers a great view for each spacious room, with expansive bathrooms to boot. It is a modern luxury in the heart of traditional Kyoto.

- Suiran Hotel (Saga-Tenryuji, Ukyo-ku, 12 Susukinobaba-cho)

Contact number: +81 75 872 0101

Aptly defined as a Luxury Collection Hotel, Suiran is by the river and is also stands on a section of the Tenryuji Temple grounds. The overall motif is traditional, granting its guests a quintessentially Kyoto experience.

- Hoshinoya Kyoto Hotel (Genrokuzancho 11-2 Arashiyama, Nishikio-ku)

Contact number: +81 50 3786 0066

This exquisite hotel can be accessed via a private boat ride, and upon arrival, guests get to experience the best of traditional Kyoto and its natural scenery.

- Rihga Royal Hotel (Horikawa-shiokoji, Shimogyo-ku)

Contact number: +81 6 6448 1121

Guests can experience the comforts of modern amenities and the charm of traditional Kyoto in this classic luxury hotel.

Chapter 5: Osaka

Osaka is the second biggest metropolitan area in Japan and one of the largest in the entire world. During the Edo period, the locals called Osaka *tenka no daidokoro* or the *nation's kitchen*, because it was a merchant city, particularly in the rice trade.

Two rough divisions comprise Central Osaka: the downtown area or the *north* (which locals call *Kita*), and the uptown area, or the *south* (*Minami*). The Umeda district can be found in Kita and it is where you can find plenty of shopping arcades. The entertainment areas, particularly the Dotonbori, and the Namba and Shinsaibashi are located in Minami.

Travelers love to shop in Osaka because it has a wide variety of shopping arcades. It is also where you can find the National Bunraku Theatre, where you can watch puppet plays. Of course, it is also the home of Universal Studio Japan and other widely popular amusement parks.

Best Times to Visit

The best time to go to Osaka is between the months of March and April (spring) because you would definitely want to enjoy the Cherry Blossom Festival. You will also enjoy May as it is when the Golden Week Festival is celebrated. Be aware, though, that all hotels and flights tend to get fully booked so make sure to prepare way ahead of time.

The summers in Osaka can get really hot, but if you want to attend the popular Tenjin Matsuri festival (between July 24 and 25), then be prepared for the heat.

Another great time to visit Osaka is between October and December mainly because of the cool temperature. Osaka rarely experiences snowfall, so the winter months do not get too cold, although the temperature does tend to dip around January and February.

Where to Go and What to See

Osaka Rekishi Hakubutsukan (Osaka Museum of History)

Head over to the Osaka Museum of History to immerse yourself in the history of this amazing city. The museum boasts wonderful collections of artifacts dating back to pre-feudal times and through to the early twentieth century. Perfect for visitors of all ages, the museum has several life-sized displays and a number of hands-on activities for kids and adults. For those on a strict timeframe, go along the Highlight Course, a pathway that takes you through Osaka's history in less than 60 minutes. For those with more times, check out the Complete Course, where you can enjoy the full experience.

Hours:

0930 to 1700 (until 2000 on Fridays)
Admission ends 30 minutes before closing

Closed:

Tuesday (or following day if Tuesday is a national holiday)
28th December – 4th January

Admission Fee:

600 yen

How to Get Here:

4-1-32 Otemae, Chuo-ku, Osaka 540-0008, Osaka Prefecture. Located on the southwest corner of Osaka Castle Park, the closest train stations are Tanimachi 4-chome Station and the Morinomiya Station. From here it is a five-minute walk away.

Osaka Shiritsu Toyo Toji Bijutsukan (Museum of Oriental Ceramics)

The Museum of Oriental Ceramics is situated within Naka-no-shima Koen, the oldest park within the city. Inside, the museum boasts an interesting collection of ceramics from Japan, Korea and China. The collection is made up of over 900 pieces, 15 of which are registered as National Treasures or Important Cultural Properties, making it one of the most awesome collections around the globe.

Hours:

0930 – 1630 Tuesday to Sundays

Closed:

Mondays

Admission Fee:

500 yen

How to Get Here:

1-1-26 Nakanoshima, Kita-ku, Osaka 530-0005, Osaka Prefecture. Take the train to Naniwabashi Station or to Yodoyabashi Station; from both it is a five-minute walk away.

Osaka-jo (Osaka Castle)

Osaka Castle is the city's number one attraction and it isn't hard to see why. The castle dates back to the latter part of the 16th century but the building you see before you is a reconstruction finished in 1931. The five-story high castle is now an outstanding museum dedicated to the history of the man who created the original, Hideyoshi Toyotomi, the chief royal minister who brought the country together again.

The castle features beautiful exhibitions of artifacts and artworks but for those who enjoy something more visual, head to the tower where you can indulge in awe-inspiring views over the city. The best time to visit Osaka Castle is just before sunset – the views of the nearby park as the setting sun drenches it in a hue of gold, red and pinks is certainly worth it.

Hours:

0900 to 1700 (entrance until 1630)
Extended hours during various holidays and special exhibitions.

Closed:

28th December to 1st January

Admission Fee:

600 yen

How to Get Here:

Osakajo, Chuoku, Osaka 540-0002, Osaka Prefecture. The closest train station to Osaka Castle Park is Tanimachi 4-chome Station or Osakajokoen Station. From both it is a short ten minute walk to the park.

Sumiyoshi Taisha (Sumiyoshi Grand Shrine)

As a coastal city, it is little wonder then that the patron god of sailors has long been popular. Sumiyoshi Taisha is a shrine dedicated to the god and is said to have been founded by Empress Jingu in 211 as gratitude for her safe return from Korea. Sumiyoshi Taisha is one of three shrines constructed before Buddhist was introduced into Japan (the others beinng Ise Jingu in Mie Prefecture and Izumo Taisha in Tottori Prefecture). It has long been traditional In Shintoism to de-construct and rebuilt shrines at certain times in the same way as the original. The one you see today dates back to 1810. Look out for the arched bridge, a gift from Yodo-gimi, a consort of Hideoshi Toyotomi, with whom she had a son.

A great time to visit Sumiyoshi Taisha is on the 14th June. At 1pm, the rice-picking festival begins, including processions and cultural performances. Between the 30th July and 1st August, the Sumiyoshi Matsuri takes place; this vibrant festival includes the procession of a two-ton moveable shrine carried from the main shrine to Yamato-gawa and then brought back and then followed by a bazaar, which stays open all night.

Hours:

0600 – 1700 April to September

0630 – 1700 October to March

Admission Fee:

Free

How to Get Here:

2-9-89 Sumiyoshi, Sumiyoshi-ku, Osaka 558-0045, Osaka Prefecture. The shrine is located adjacent to the Sumiyoshi Taisha Station.

Tenno-ji Koen (Tenno-ji Park)

Tenno-ji Koen is a haven of peace and tranquility as well as the home of the Municipal Museum of Fine Art, the Tenno-ji Botannical Gardens, the Keitaku-en garden, and the prehistorical burial mound of Chausuyama Kofun, the place where Tokugawa Ieyasu and his army camped during the siege of Osaka Castle in 1614 – 1615. The best time to visit is during the early morning or evenings when it is quieter.

Admission Fee:

Free

How to Get Here:

1_108 Chausuyamacho, Tennoji-ku, Osaka 543-0063, Osaka Prefecture. The park is a few steps away from the Tennji Train Station.

Nightlife

Whatever you want in nightlife, Osaka has it. When the sun goes down, the city comes to life, with a wide range of bars, restaurants, clubs and theatres. Visitors can enjoy a variety of cultural and contemporary performances before heading out to a club or bar.

Cinquecento

Located in Shinsaibashi, Cinquecento is a groovy shot bar boasting a fun atmosphere and great service. The food is limited in range but the martini menu is second to none and there are a variety of beers you can sample.

How to Get Here:

1F 2-1-10 Higashi Shinsaibashi, Chuo-ku, Osaka
Tel: (06) 6213 6788.

Fubar

Fubar is a fun and funky sports bar that serves a variety of foods, cocktails and draft beers. Get your groove on up on the second floor dance area where guest DJs come and play at the weekends. However, the rest of the time it is visited by customers who want to watch broadcasts of football.

How to Get Here:

2F 1-5-2 Shinsaibashi-suji, Chuo-ku, Osaka
Tel: (06) 6245 3757.

The Blarney Stone

The Blarney Stone is a popular Irish pub within the center of Umeda that features live performances, pool and other pub games. Enjoy a pint of Guinness or any of the other international ales and beers. This is an ideal place to go if you fancy pie and mash or traditional fish and chips.

How to Get Here:

2-10-15 Sonezaki, Kita-ku, Osaka
Tel: (06) 6364 2001.

Club Karma

On Friday and Saturday nights, Club Karma plays hosts to a number of international DJs. Whilst it's rather plain inside, it does feature a good food selection and Happy Hour until 9pm.

How to Get Here:

B1 1-5-18 Sonezaki-Shinchi, Kita-ku, Osaka
Tel: (06) 6344 6181.

Joule

Located within the vibrant Shinsaibashi area, Joule is a popular club that plays mainstream music where you can get your groove on upon the large dance floor. Head upstairs to the third floor to relax within the lounge when you need to rest your feet.

How to Get Here:

2, 3, 4F 2-11-7 Nishi-Shinsaibashi, Chuo-ku, Osaka
Tel: (06) 6214 1223.

Where and What to Eat

Must-Try: Sushi, Takoyaki, Okonomiyaki, Taiko Manjuu, Kushikatsu, Yakiniku

Budget

- Kougaryu

One of the most popular takoyaki joints in Osaka is this restaurant. They serve fast, affordable and delicious takoyaki, which you can enjoy as a snack or as a cheap lunch, if you are on a diet.

- Gozasoro

Taiko manjuu is a traditional dessert or snack in Japan made of red bean paste mochi. It is grilled, resulting in ooey gooey goodness. Get the best traditional kind from from this shop, which you can find in mall food areas.

- 298

How much shabu shabu and yakiniku can you eat within 90 minutes? Well, it should be a lot because that is what you will get from this restaurant for a low price!

- Yamamoto

Looking for okonomiyaki? Visit this restaurant in Yodogawa-ku. Their specialty is Negiyaki, which is made of spring onions in batter and their secret sauce.

- Zuboraya (2-5-5, Ebisu higashi, Naniwa-ku, Osaka City)

As you tour the streets of Osaka, you would not miss the gigantic globefish sign of this restaurant. They serve hotpot dishes at fair prices, and their specialty is -no surprise here- fresh globefish sashimi and hotpot.

- Osaka Ohsho

This Chinese-Japanese restaurant is a big deal in Osaka, and their specialty is handmade gyoza.

High End

- Hajime (1-9-11-1, Edobori, Nishi-ku, Osaka-City)

The chef and owner, Hajime Yonekda, has every right to be proud of this French restaurant because in less than two years after it opened, it immediately got three Michelin stars.

- Fujiya 1935 (2-4-14, Yariyamachi, Chuo-ku, Osaka City)

This Spanish-style restaurant first opened its doors in 2003 and has earned three Michelin stars in 2012. Only the freshest seasonal ingredients are used in the various dishes they serve. When you choose a dish, you may opt to accompany it with the wine that they recommend.

- Saeki (Mori building 1F, 1-5-7, Sonezaki shinchi, Kita-ku, Osaka-City0)

Do you want to eat the best sushi in Osaka? Head over to this restaurant! It has an overall opulent ambiance and provides its customers with the wonderful experience of witnessing the chef prepare the sushi right before their eyes.

- Mizuno (1-4-15, Dotonbori, Chuo-ku, Osaka City)

This Okonomiyaki restaurant has been standing strong since 1945, making it the oldest one in Japan. Many diners love their Yam Okonomiyaki, otherwise called *yamaimo-yaki*, so that is definitely a must-try.

Where to Stay

Low Budget

- City Route Hotel (2-3-6 Utsubohonmachi, Nishi-ku)

Contact number: +81 06 6448 1000

Stretch your budget and stay in Osaka by checking into this hotel. Its location will also save you time and money as it is a walk away from Shinsaibashi shopping area and plenty of great, affordable restaurants.

- Hotel Kinki (17-8 Kita-ku Doyama-cho)

Contact number: +81 6 6312 9117

The hotel's name is a bit of a pun as is located close to the red light district. Nevertheless, travelers will feel safe staying here and the hotel itself is clean and conveniently close to many shops and restaurants.

- Dotonbori Hotel (2-3-25 Dotombori, Chuo-ku)

Contact number: +81 6 6213 9040

This hotel is not just budget-friendly, but also extremely convenient because it is just a 10 minute walk from Namba Station. And although the rooms are small, they are also extremely neat and clean.

- Toyoko Inn Hankyu Jusoeki Nishiguchi (1-13-4 Jusohonmachi, Yodogawa-ku)

Contact number: +81 6 6313 1045

Clean rooms, complete amenities, and friendly staff... What more can you ask for from a budget hotel? Bonus: it is also close to the Juso Station.

- Business Hotel Mikado (1-2-11, Taishi, Nishinari-ku)

Contact number: +81 6 6647 1355

This budget hotel is a stone's throw away from the Dobutsuen-Mae subway station and Nankai railway station. It offers small but clean and very affordable rooms.

Mid-range Budget

- Hotel New Hankyu (1-1-35 Shibata 1, Kita-ku)

Contact number: +81 6 6372 5101

This reasonably-priced hotel is popular because of its great location: it is close to the Osaka Castle, the Science Museum, and the Shinsaibashi Shopping Arcade, to mention a few.

- Hotel Monterey Grasmere (1-2-3 Minatomachi, Naniwa-ku)

Contact number: +81 6 6645 7111

This romantic hotel offers clean, comfortable rooms and easy access to the Tsutenkaku Tower, Shitennoji Temple, and Shinsaibashi Shopping Arcade.

- Hotel Granvia (3-1-1 Umeda, Kita-ku)

Contact number: +81 6 6344 1235

This hotel is literally located right above the JR Osaka station, which makes it highly convenient for travelers who want to get lost in the city.

High End

- Intercontinental Hotel (3-60 Ofuka-Cho Kita-Ku)

Contact number: +81 6 6374 5700

This is a 5-star hotel that is perfect for those who want to have a highly luxurious experience in Osaka. The rooms are expansive and offer a jaw-dropping view.

- Osaka Marriott Miyako Hotel (1-1-43 Abenosuji, Abeno-ku,)

Contact number: +81 6 6628 6111

Nobody who checks into this grand hotel is ever disappointed. It boasts of fantastic and generously spacious rooms and impeccable service.

- The St. Regis Hotel (3-6-12 Hommachi, Chuo-ku)

Contact number: +81 6 6258 3333

This sophisticated hotel with its elegant and deeply comfortable rooms is perfect for those who want to shop in Osaka because it is only a station away from Shinsaibashi and two stations away from Namba.

- Fraser Residence Nankai (1-17-11 Nambanaka, Naniwa-ku)

Contact number: +81 6 6635 7111

Aside from the usual comforts and amenities that you can find in high end hotels, this one is best known for its perfect location: it is right across the Nankai station and the Takashimaya shopping area.

- The Ritz-Carlton Osaka (2-5-25 Umeda, Kita-ku)

Contact number: +81 6 6343 7000

Do you want to live in opulence during your stay in Osaka? Check into this 5-star hotel and get exactly what you are craving for. Some travelers have even claimed that their stay became the highlight of their trip.

Chapter 6: Yokohama

What was once a small fishing village, Yokohama is now home to 3.7 million people, garnering it the second biggest city after Tokyo as far as population is concerned. The city lies on Tokyo Bay and it serves as a main commercial center of the Greater Tokyo Area. It is primarily identified as a port city.

Yokohama is also where you can find the tallest inland lighthouse in the world, the Yokohama Marine Tower. There, you can also find the so-called *world's biggest clock*, which is actually a Ferris wheel called Cosmo Clock 21. Studio Ghibli fans might want to visit the Yamate district of the city because it is where the movie *From Up on Poppy Hill* was set.

Best Times to Visit

As far as weather is concerned, the best time would be in the months of March to May (spring) and September to November (fall). Among the not-so-great times to visit are around the months of June and July because of the constant rain.

The festivals celebrated in Yokohama are the same as those in Tokyo, with special events taking place every year. Because of the dynamic nature of their festival events, you can find out what to expect by searching for the latest updates on the internet.

Where to Go and What to See

Yokohama Chinatown

Established in 1863, Yokohama's Chinatown is the largest of its kind in the entire country. As you can imagine, you will find a wide range of Chinese shops, restaurants and cafes, along with a number of individual sites and attractions to visit. The main entrances boasts four Chinese-style gates and five more gates within the area.

Chinatown was established during the latter part of the Edo Period; at this time, Yokohama was established as Treaty Port and continued to prosper through the Meiji Period. It was this time when many Chinese migrants, mostly from Canton (modern-day Guangzhou) Hong Kong, started to arrive. Shops and restaurants began construction, along with the Chinese temple, also known as the Kantei-byo Shrine, a school and community center.

The Kantei-byo Shrine was built in honor of Guan Yu, a Chinese warlord and the patron of the two thousand Chinese people who live in the city. Pay special attention to the intricately decorated gateways – they are a photo shoot just by themselves.

During the early 20th century, Chinatown suffered many issues. In 1923, the Great Kanto Earthquake caused much damage and then the China-Japanese War in the 1930s meant that the relationship between the two was hostile. However, after the war, Chinatown was awarded official status in the mid-1950s and since the 1970s, Chinatown has become a popular tourist area.

Hours:

Always open.

Admission Fee:

Free.

How to Get Here:

118_2 Yamashitacho, Naka-ku, Yokohama 231-0023, Kanagawa Prefecture. The closest train stations to Chinatown are Motomachi-Chukagai Station and Ishikawacho Stations, which take around seven or eight minutes from Yokohama Station.

Minato Mirai 21

Minato Mirari 21, also referred to as MM21, is a district that features a number of attractions for visitors to enjoy. Landmark Tower is certainly one of the best sites to visit. Standing at 296 meters high, it was constructed in the 1990s; head up to the 69th floor where you can enjoy panoramic views over the city from the Sky Garden. But don't worry about climbing all those stairs - it has the fastest elevator in the world to take you up there.

Be sure to look out for the Pacifico Yokohama, a massive conference center that looks somewhat like a giant sail in the wind. It also houses the Yokohama Grand Intercontinental Hotel.

Pay a visit to the Yokohama Maritime Museum; the world famous sailing ship from the early 20th century, the Nippon Maru, is here. After exploring the many exhibitions on show here, head to the Cosmo Clock Ferris Wheel, one of the biggest Ferris wheels in the world. It is situated on Shinko-cho Island and can hold 480 people at a time at 112.5 meters high.

Queen's Square Complex on the island is great for shopaholics as well as those searching for a bite to eat. You will also discover the Yokohama Minato Hall here where classical music shows are performed.

Hours:

All hours.

Admission Fee:

Free, entrance fees vary per each individual attraction.

How to Get Here:

The best train station to get off at is the Minato Mirai Station which takes you to the heart of the area.

Kanagawa Prefectural Museum

Located within the old Yokohama Specie Bank, the Kanagawa Prefectural Museum is a great place to go if you are interested in getting to know the local history. The building itself dates back to the turn of the 20th century, and the well-laid out exhibitions are full of interesting artifacts from all eras.

Hours:

0900 – 1630

Closed:

Mondays.

29th December – 1st January.

Admission Fee:

510 yen

How to Get Here:

5-60 Minami-Nakadori, Yokohama 231-0006, Kanagawa Prefecture. The museum is three minutes walk away from Iriuda Station.

Yokohama Foreigners' Cemetery

As a Treaty Port, Yokohama was the home of many foreigners. Between the mid-19th century to the present, nearly 5,000 foreigners from Europe and America have been interred at the Yokohama Foreigner's Cemetery. There are several historical celebrities here, including Charles Richardson who was repeatedly struck by samurai in 1862, and Edward Morel, the principal engineer who helped the established first railway in Japan.

Hours:

1200 – 1600 on weekends

Closed:

Weekdays and between January and February

Admission Fee:

Donation.

How to Get Here:

96 Yamate-cho, Yokohama, Kanagawa Prefecture. The closest train station to the cemetery is Motomachi-Chukagai Station, or else you can get off at the Ishikawacho Station.

Yokohama Doll Museum

The Yokohama Doll Museum is located on the southeast part of Yamashita-koen, opposite the Harbor View Park and has an amazing collection of dolls. Here you will discover thousands upon thousands of dolls from all over the world, including a fantastic display of *hina* dolls from Japan.

Hours:

1000 – 1630 Tuesdays to Sundays

<u>Closed</u>:

Mondays and public holidays.

<u>Admission Fee:</u>

400 yen.

<u>How to Get Here</u>:

18 Yamashita-cho, Naka-ku, Yokohama 231-0023, Kanagawa Prefecture. It is a short walk to the museum from Ishikawacho Station and Motomachi-Chukagai Station.

Yokohama Marine Tower

The Yokohama Marine Tower is close to the Yokohama Doll Museum. Standing at 106-meter-high, visitors can enjoy impressive vistas over the city, the sea and Yamashita Park. It opened in 1961 and features a restaurant and a bar.

<u>Hours</u>:

1000 – 2230

<u>Admission Fee</u>:

750 yen.

<u>How to Get Here</u>:

15 Yamashitacho, Yokohama 231-0023, Kanagawa Prefecture. Motomachi-Chinatown station, exit #4 and walk for 1 minute.

Yokohama Museum of Art

The city boasts several museums but the Yokohama Museum of Art, close to the Yokohama Marine Tower, is second to none. Most of the pieces found inside the building, designed by Kenzo Tange, were created after 1859 when the city was established. The museum is especially renowned for its excellent collection of Surrealist and modern arts, in addition to its displays of photographs.

Hours:

1000 - 1800 (last admission at 1730)

Closed:

Thursdays and 28th January to 1st January.

Admission Fee:

500 yen for collections.

Admission to exhibitions vary.

How to Get Here:

3-4-1, Mintomirai, Nishi-ku, Yokohama 220-0012, Kanagawa Prefecture. It is a three-minute walk from the Minatomirai Station, or a ten-minute walk from Sakuragicho Station. For those coming via bus, take the Yokohama Municipal Bus Route Number 156 or 292 from Sakuragicho Station, and get off at Yokohama-bijutsukan.

Mitsubishi Minatomirai Industrial Museum

Located behind the Yokohama Museum of Art, this is a great museum for boys who like their toys. Here, you can see a rocket engine, go on a helicopter simulator and explore an ocean submarine.

Hours:

1000 – 1700 (last entry at 1630)

Closed:

Tuesdays and New Year holidays

Admission Fee:

500 yen

How to Get Here:

3-3-1 Minatomirai, Nishi-ku | Mitsubishijuko Yokohama Building, Yokohama 220-0012, Kanagawa Prefecture. From the Minato Mirai Station, it is a five minute walk to the museum.

Nightlife

Due to its location by the sea and as the second biggest city in Japan, the nightlife in Yokohama is second to only Tokyo. You'll discover a vibrant and pulsating energy to the city when the sun goes down, with numerous nightclubs, bars, restaurants and other entertainment venues to enjoy.

Thrashzone Yokohama

Thrashzone is a fast-paced club which features strong beer and even stronger heavy metallic music. However, it is one of the friendliest and most relaxing places you could visit in the evening. Don't forget to try the Belgium fries – they are certainly a treat for the taste buds.

Hours:

1200 – 2330

How to Get Here:

Address: 1F Tamura bldg, 2-10-7 Tsuruya-cho, Nishi-ku, Yokohama. Telephone: +81 45-514-9947

Sky Café

Located on the 69th floor of the Landmark Tower, guests can enjoy outstanding views of the city as they dine and sip on a variety of cocktails, wines, beers and spirits. Both romantic and atmospheric, you can even see as far as Tokyo Bay. The Sky Café is great for those who want to socialize in a vibrant yet peaceful setting with great service.

Hours:

1000 – 2100

1000 – 2200 Saturdays

How to Get Here:

69F The Landmark Tower Yokohama, 2-1-1, Minatomirai 2-chome, Nishi-ku,Yokohama. Telephone: +81 45-222-5031

Belgian Beer and Grill Glass Dance

Searching for something different? Then head over to the Belgian Beer and Grill Glass Dance. Here, guests can sample 70 different Belgian beers and equally as many draft beers. Combine it with a variety of various dishes from all over the world and great music, and you have the perfect setting for a memorable night out.

How to Get Here:

9fl., Yokohama More's, 1-3-1, Minamisaiwai, Nishi-ku, Yokohama, 220-8533. Telephone: +81 45-311-0278

Where and What to Eat

Must-Try: Gyunabe, Sanma-men, Nikuman

Budget

- Shitateya

This restaurant is famous among the young ones due to its highly affordable options. Choose their seafood dishes as they are deemed the best, such as the deep fried oysters, or *kaki furai*.

- Shabu-Shabu Buffet Shiabu-Yo

You can find this restaurant in Minato Mirai. Although it is not the cheapest place to eat in, the atmosphere and all-you-can-eat shabu shabu are well worth it.

- Tori Dori

This popular restaurant is known for its yakitori, or grilled chicken. They also serve all-you-can-drink beer.

- Hello Kitty Cafe

It would be sacrilegious to not mention this cafe when you are planning to go to Yokohama, especially if you are a big fan of its billion-dollar icon.

High End

- Baikotei (Baikotei, 1 Chome-1 Aioicho, Naka Ward)

This pre-World War II restaurant is a living legend in Yokohama. It has managed to preserve its charming antique interiors, down to the worn out seats and the creaking wooden floors. A must-try is the hayashi and beef onion stew.

- Manchinro Honten (Manchinro Honten, 153 Yamashitacho, Naka Ward)

Since 1892, this Cantonese restaurant in Yokohama Chinatown is one place you should never skip going to if you have the budget for fine dining. One popular dish on the menu is the crab meat parcel, although dumplings are the specialty of the house.

- Azamino Ukai-tei

This sophisticated French-Japanese restaurant offers its luxurious surroundings and mouthwatering delicacies to any traveler who wants to live the high life. Their Kobe beef and steaks are widely lauded.

Where to Stay

Low Budget

- Toyoko Inn Yokohama Sakuragi-cho (6-55 Honcho Naka-ku)

Contact number: +81 45 671 1045

This budget hotel may have small rooms, but the amenities provide wonderful comfort. Visit the 69th floor to capture a great view of Mt Fuji.

- Hotel Wing International Yokohama Kannai (1-2 Furocho, Naka-ku)

Contact number: +81 45 681 4800

This consistently comfortable and clean budget-friendly hotel provides all the basics you need during your stay. It is only a minute's walk away from JR Kannai station, making it a convenient place to stay in for business and leisure.

- Comfort Hotel Yokohama Kannai (3-33 Sumiyoshicho, Naka-ku)

Contact number: +81 45 650 4711

This affordable hotel is conveniently located close to Kannai station. The rooms, although small, are clean and comfortable, and the staff are quite accommodating and friendly.

- Sotetsu Fresa Inn (16-8 Totsukacho, Totsuka-ku)

Contact number: +81 45 640 0203

This hotel is perfect for those who want to go sightseeing but are on a budget. It is conveniently close to the Yokohama Station and just three stops from Kamakura Station. Buses can easily be taken from the hotel to get to Totsuka area.

Mid-range Budget

- Sakuragicho Washington Hotel (1-101-1 Sakuragi-cho, Naka-ku)

Contact number: +81 45 683 3111

This highly affordable 3-star hotel is widely recommended as it is close to most of the top destinations in the city, such as the Landmark Tower, Yokohama Museum of Art, and Cosmo World.

- Shin Yokohama Prince Hotel (3-4 Shin Yokohama, Kohoku-ku)

Contact number: +81 45 471 1111

This romantic hotel offers clean and comfortable rooms at reasonable prices. It is a mere 10-minute walk away from Yokohama Arena and Shinyokohama Raumen Museum.

- Hotel Monterey (6-1 Yamashita-cho, Naka-ku)

Contact number: +81 45 330 7111

This reasonably priced romantic hotel is located close to the Yamashita Park and the Osanbashi International Passenger Terminal. If you want a harbor view from your room, book the Standard Twin Rooms.

High End

- InterContinental Yokohama Grand (1-1-1 Minato Mirai, Nishi-ku)

Contact number: +81 45 223 2222

This gorgeous luxury hotel is close to the Minatomirai Station and provides its guests with a great view of the Ferris Wheel.

- The Yokohama Bay Hotel Tokyu (2-3-7 Minatomirai Nishi-ku)

Contact number: +81 45 682 2222

Located at the heart of Yokohama, this high-end hotel has the Certificate of Excellence with its impeccable rooms and service as well as breathtaking view.

- Yokohama Royal Park Hotel (2-2-1-3 Minatomirai, Nishi-Ku)

Contact number: +81 45 221 1111

Lovely and spacious rooms, a delectable buffet, and a superb location, this classically designed hotel is perfect for travelers who only want the best.

- Hotel New Grand (10 Yamashiracho, Naka-ku)

Contact number: +81 45 681 1841

Despite its name, this luxury hotel has been standing strong since 1927 and is a favorite among seasoned travelers and neophytes alike. World War II buffs will get an experience of a lifetime in this hotel as it houses the exact same desk where General MacArthur once sat in.

- Hotel Yokohama Garden (254 Yamashitacho, Naka-ku)

Contact number: +81 45 641 1311

Looking for a high end hotel with a fantastic location? This one is highly recommended. It is walking distance to most of the major attractions in the city, such as Osanbashi Pier, Yamashita Park, and Chinatown.

Chapter 7: Fukuoka

Fukuoka is in the northern part of Kyushu and is regarded as the sixth largest city in Japan. In 2006, it was named as one of the ten most Dynamic Cities in the World by Newsweek. Because of its close proximity to central Asia, its economy boomed in terms of trade and tourism. You can even say that the place is a melting pot of cultures.

Fukuoka may be not be as popular as the other main cities in this guide, but that is the beauty of it as well. In fact, many Japanese people can argue that it is one of the best cities to live in. If you happen to pass by, you will discover fantastic boutiques, a wide variety of restaurants to choose from across the low and high-end spectrum, and possibly enjoy the best bowl of ramen you have ever eaten.

Best Times to Visit

Fall season (September to October) may be the best time to go to Fukuoka because the weather would be pleasantly cool. However, if you want to witness the trees in full bloom then you should be there in spring (March to April).

From September 12 to 18 is the Hojoya festival in Hakozaki Shrine where everyone visits the shrines to give thanks for the rich autumn harvest. The Asian Month Festival is held throughout the same month in Fukuoka City. On the first Thursday, Friday, and Saturday of October is the Nakasu Festival, another celebratory thanksgiving feast.

If you are there in November, you can check out the Kyushu Grand Sumo Tournament held in Fukuoka Kokusai Center. On the first Sunday of December, you might want to see the Fukuoka International Open Marathon Championship in Heiwadai Stadium, which is a world-class marathon competition.

January and February are winter months in Fukuoka, but the temperature rarely goes to subzero, so you can still go out and enjoy.

On January 3, the Tamaseseri festival is held, which is an interesting ritualistic one involving men in loincloths fighting for a ball. Between January 8 to 11 is the Toka Ebisu festival dedicated to the god of fishery, Ebisu. On February 3rd is the Setsubun Festival, is celebrated on the last day of winter.

The first Sunday of March is when people celebrate the Kyokusui no en where you can witness an old shrine ritual that involves an attendant composing a poem right before a flowing bowl of sake gets overfilled.

Between May 3 and 4 is the Hakata Dontaku Port festival where there is a huge parade along Meiji Street.

July 1 to 15 is the Hakata Gion Yamasaka in Kushida Shrine, while on August 1, you can witness the Nishinihon Ohori Fireworks Festival in Ohori Park.

Where to Go and What to See

Canal City

Canal City is a district perfect for those who love to shop, dine and people watch in a vibrant atmosphere. Choose from any one of the numerous restaurants on offer here, ranging from budget to fine dining, before browsing at the many stores. There is a massive IMAX cinema here for those who want to take in a movie or two. On one end of the shopping areas is a water display area that spurts up to the tune from the Indiana Jones movie. On the opposite side is a half dome building decked out in pale pinks and blues with oodles of glass, featuring balconies with stores and cafes, making it one of the most striking shopping areas you will ever come across.

Hours:

1000 – 2100 (restaurants until 2300)

Shops vary.

Admission Fee:

Free

How to Get Here:

1-2 Sumiyoshi, Hakata-ku, Fukuoka 812-0018, Fukuoka Prefecture. You can take a short loop bus from Tenjin Station or Hakata Station or you can walk for 20 minutes or 15 minutes respectively from these stations.

Ohori Koen

This delightful and charming park used to be part of the moat that encased Fukuoka's castle. In early April, the park blooms into a hue of pink and white when the 2,600 cherry trees blossom, creating a glorious spectacle. It is within Ohori Koen that you will discover the Fukuoka City Art Museum, which boasts artworks from Dali, Warhol, Miro and Chagall, among other prominent artists.

<u>Hours:</u>

0900 – 1700

<u>Closed:</u>

Mondays

<u>Admission Fee:</u>

240 yen

<u>How to Get Here:</u>

1-2 Ohorikoen, Chuo-ku, Fukuoka 810-0051, Fukuoka Prefecture. The park is situated a stone's throw from Ohori Koen Subway Station, or a ten-minute walk from Hakata Station.

Shofuku-ji (Shofuku Temple)

Eisai (1141 – 1215) was a monk who spent a considerable amount of time in China before returning home to Japan and introducing Zen Buddhism and planting the very first tea-bush seeds here. While tea is grown in various parts of Japan, the tea grown here is considered special and is sold all over the country. In addition to planting tea bushes, the monk also founded the first Zen Buddhist temple, Shofuku-ji, which is recorded on the main gates by Emperor Gotoba. The setting of the temple is calm and peaceful, a reflection of the philosophy of Zen traditions and the temple itself is quite stunning. Head up to the belfry where the bronze bell sits – it was proclaimed an Important Cultural Property – and the views are impressive and mesmerizing.

<u>Hours:</u>

Always open.

Admission Fee:

Free.

How to Get Here:

6-1 Gokushomachi, Hakata-ku, Fukuoka 812-0037, Fukuoka Prefecture. The temple is within a short distance from the Gion Station, or 20 minutes away from Hakata Station.

Iwataya

For those who like to shop until they drop, head to Iwataya. This multi-level department store sells a variety of goods including silks, ceramics and Hakata dolls.

Admission Fee:

Free.

How to Get Here:

2-5-35, Tenjin, Chuo-ku, Fukuoka 810-8680, Fukuoka Prefecture. From Tenjin Station it is a short walk to Iwataya.

Kawabata Shotengai (Kawabata Shopping Arcade)

The Kawabata Shopping Arcade boasts restaurants and stores reminiscent of the Edo era, where you can purchase a variety of merchandise and souvenirs, stretching from the Nakasu-Kawabata subway station all the way to Canal City.

Admission Fee:

Free.

How to Get Here:

Kamikawabatamachi Hakata-ku, Fukuoka 812-0026, Fukuoka Prefecture. Close to the Kushida Shrine, the shopping arcade is a 10 minute walk from Nakasukawabata Station.

Nightlife

During the day, Fukuoka is a charming coastal city somewhat reminiscent of the Edo period boasting mountains, beaches, quaint cultural attractions and many shopping areas. However, once the sun sets, the fun side of the city comes out with the stars. You'll discover quite a different side to Fukuoka, a place full of energy and vibrancy.

There are a vast number of restaurants, cafes, bars, clubs and other entertainment venues to choose from. Whether you're in the mood to dance the night away or to socialize in a quieter, more elegant setting, you'll discover it all here.

Android Bar

Android Bar is a hip underground bar with a science fiction neo-Japanese flair offering great music and an even better selection of drinks. Relax in one of the comfortable chairs or sofas as you peruse the menu as you listen to a range of music performances. Smoking is permitted here.

How to Get Here:

11-1 Shin-kawabata Building, B1F Hakata-ku, Fukuoka, 812-0026, Tel: 00 81 92 291 276.

Blue Bar

Blue, blue, blue – expect nothing else but this color in Blue Bar. Decked out in various shades of blue, from the iciest hue to the most electric shade of blue, you'll feel as though you're in an underwater or an alien paradise here. The lighting effect really enhances the atmosphere as you decide on what you fancy sipping on.

How to Get Here:

3-7-10 Wakamatsu Building, Fukuoka, Fukuoka Prefecture, 810-0801. Telephone: +81 (0)92 262 2002

Misty

Searching for something calmer and more relaxing? Look no further than Misty. Stylish and elegant, this is an ideal setting for socializing with friends or romancing someone special. Work your way through the impressive drink menu, which features delectable cocktails, spirits and wines and enjoy the atmosphere.

How to Get Here:

Oak Building 4F 2-18-15, Kego, Chuo-ku, Fukuoka, 810 0023. Telephone: 00 81 (0)92 751 9495

O/D

O/D is a stylish place that has been decorated with a minimalist feel in mind. You will find O/D's to be a fun place to dance the night away to a variety of musical genres played by local DJs, with an emphasis on hip hop and soul.

How to Get Here:

Tokyo Troy Building 4F, 1-1-10 Maizuru, Chuo-ku, Fukuoka. Telephone: (00 8192) 733 1166

Ritz Spooky Mix

Expect high-tech, great music and drinks galore at Ritz Spooky Mix. Here you can enjoy a range of music played as loud as your eardrums can take, with each night different from the last. DJs change frequently and it is an incredibly popular place to get your groove on.

How to Get Here:

Dai 8 Line Building. 5th floor 2-4-19, Tenjin. Fukuoka. Telephone: (00 8192) 715 8376

The Happy Cock

The Happy Cock Bar is popular with the younger locals and tourists. During the weekends it can get incredibly crowded, the music even louder, and the atmosphere buzzing. Choose from a wide range of drinks and food to enjoy as you try to keep your feet from moving.

How to Get Here:

9F Neo Palace ll Building,2-1-51 Daimyo, Fukuoka. Telephone: 00 8192 734 3686

Where and What to Eat

Must-Try: Ramen, Tonkotsu, Motsunabe, Udon, Gyoza, Fugu

Budget

- Tempura no Hirao Tenjin Restaurant

This restaurant is famous for... You guessed it. Tempura! The prices are not intimidating at all, and it is also easy to find as it is located in the center of Tenjin shopping district.

- Ippudo Daimyo Restaurant

For tasty ramen on a budget, visit this restaurant, which now has many branches across and outside Japan.

- Food Stalls in Nakasu

Since you are in Fukuoka, you should find *Nakasu*, which is a spot located in between Naka River and Hakata River. Plenty of food stalls sell all sorts of inexpensive tempura, yakitori, oden, and ramen among others. There's alcohol, too.

High End

- Restaurant Hiramatsu Hakata (Hakata Riverain 2F, 3-1, Shimo-Kawabatamachi, Hakata-ku)

This top quality French restaurant has been around for close to three decades now. Run by Fukuoka native, chef Hiroyuki Hiramatsu, it offers different fresh seasonal food with the traditional French flaire.

- Yamanaka (2-8-8 Watanabe doori, Chuo-ku, Fukuokashi)

To get authentic *Hakata-mae* sushi, you should head over this high end restaurant. Its chic modern interior by world renowned architect, Arata Isozaki, adds to even more glamour to the overall dining experience.

Where to Stay

Low Budget

- Toyoko Inn Hakata-guchi Ekimae (1-15-5 Hakataekimae, Hakataku)

Contact number: +81 92 437 1045

What makes this budget hotel great is its location: to get to Hakata Station, all you have to do is take the underpass or go up through the overhead bridge.

- Hakata Green Hotel Tenjin (2-9-11 Daimyo, Chuoku)

Contact number: +81 92 722 3636

Despite the rooms being small (as expected of any budget hotel in Japan), the accommodations are clean and comfortable and the wifi fast.

- Dormy Inn Hakata Gion (1-12 Reisenmachi, Hakata-ku)

Contact number: +81 92 271 5489

You can get good value for your money because this budget hotel also offers a hot spring experience and the best amenities a budget hotel can offer. You can even get free ramen between 9:30 to 11:00 pm.

- Hotel Sunline Fukuoka Hakata Ekimae (4-11-18 Hakataekimae, Hakata-ku)

Contact number: +81 92 722 0033

This budget business hotel provides excellent service and great value in accommodations for a relatively low price. It is also situated near JR station.

Mid-range Budget

- Hakata Green Hotel No.1 (4-4 Hakata-eki Chuo-gai, Hakata-ku)

Contact number: +81 92 451 4111

Located in the heart of Hakata, this hotel offers reasonably priced rooms with close access to Tochoji Temple, Hakata Machiya Folk Museum, and Kushida Shrine.

- Hotel Hokke Club (3-1-90 Sumiyoshi, Hakata)

Contact number: +81 92 271 3171

This modern-style hotel is near the main Hakata Train Terminal and is equally close to the Hakata Machiya Folk Museum, Tochoji Temple, and Kushida Shrine.

High End

- Candeo Hotels The Hakata Terrace (2-4-14 Haruyoshi Chuo-ku)

Contact number: +81 92 734 0300

This highly stylish luxury hotel boasts of a great view of Canal City. The rooms are clean and modern, and the amenities are nothing short of spectacular.

- Hotel Okura (3-2 Shimokawabata-machi Hakata-ku)

Contact number: +81 92 262 1111

If you are looking for a luxury hotel in the more quiet side of the city, then this is the one you are looking for. You will be happy to know that it is near Canal City complex and Fukuoka Station.

- Hotel Nikko (2-18-25 Hakata Ekimae, Hakata-ku)

Contact number: +81 92 482 1111

This strategically located high end hotel is 3 minutes away from JR Hakata and provides spacious rooms with all the amenities needed to enjoy utmost comfort.

- Royal Park Hotel (2-14-15 Hakata-ekimae Hakata-ku)

Contact number:+852 2601 2111

Foodies and shoppers might want to book a room in this luxury hotel because it is situated right between Canal City and JR Hakata Station.

- The Luigans (18-25 Saitozaki, Higashi-ku)

Contact number: +81 92 603 2525

This beautiful, modern hotel boasts of a delightful ocean view and close access to the seaside park.

Chapter 8: Nagoya

According to some historians, the city of Nagoya got its name from the adjective *nagoyaka*, which means *peaceful*. Another name for the city is Chūkyō (meaning, *middle capital*).

Nagoya used to be, and still is, a major trading city and the political center of the most powerful house of the Tokugawa family. In particular, the rule of the 7th lord, Tokugawa Muneharu, boosted the arts and trade in the city because of his passion for plays and dramas. One of the theatres that remain standing since the feudal times is the Noh theatre at Nagoya Castle, and it continues to hold monthly performances.

If you plan on getting Japanese handicrafts, Nagoya can offer a wide variety from their industry, which is several hundreds of years old. Some of the most popular handicrafts are the festival dolls called *Sekku Ningyo*, the wooden clogs worn during the feudal era (called *geta*), and dyed silk.

Best Times to Visit

Visit Nagoya around spring (May and April) or autumn (September to October) to experience great weather and atmosphere during your stay there.

On March 3, you could witness the Girl's Day Festival, or *Hinamatsuri*, and see the different intricate ornamental dolls that represent the Imperial family on display in many homes. Between the months of March and April is when the cherry blossoms are in full bloom.

On September 9, the locals celebrate Chrysanthemum Day, which began in 910. In mid-October, you can take part in the *Nagoya* festival, which honors the Three Heroes of Nagoya. By the end of October is the Ōsu Street Performer's Festival.

If you happen to be there between November and December, you can witness the Shichi-Go-San Festival held on November 15 where children are brought to shrines to be blessed.

June and July weather may be rainy, but it is also when you can witness the *Atsuta* festival, *Tanabata* start festival, and *Minato* or Port festival.

Where to Go and What to See

Tokugawa Art Museum (Tokugawa Bijutsukan)

There are few art museums in Japan that can rival the magnificence of the Tokugawa Art Museum. Inside, the museum houses the 12th century scrolls of *The Tale of Genji*, which is generally considered the first novel in history. The scrolls are only displayed for a short time, with long intervals in-between, but even when they aren't on display, visitors can enjoy a wide range of arts and artifacts from various points in Japanese history. Marvel at various objects from the samurai class, including weapons, armor, clothing and tea ceremonial items. If the scrolls aren't available, there are still 110,000 other ancient scrolls and literary works to view in the Hosa Library rooms. Some of these date back to the eighth century. When you've finished, head outside. Tokugawaen is a charming Edo-style garden, perfect for soaking up the ambience and reflecting on your thoughts.

Hours: 1000 – 1700 (last entry at 1650)

Closed: Mondays

14th December – 4th January.

Admission Fee:

1200 yen for the museum

1350 museum and garden

How to Get Here:

1017 Tokugawa-cho, Higashi-ku, Nagoya 461-0023, Aichi Prefecture. It is a ten-minute walk from the Ozone Station to the museum, as well as from the Mijo Subway. The museum is also on the route of the Meguru loop bus, around a 40 minute journey from Nagoya Station.

Atsuta Jingu (Atsuta Shrine)

The Atsuta Jingu is the second most important Shinto shrine in Japan after Ise. There has been a shrine here for 1,700 years, which highlights its importance to the religion even in today's modern culture. Inside the Treasure House (Homotsukan) is said to be the Grass Mowing Sword, or Kusanagi-no-Tsurugi, one of the three royal regalia used by the emperor. However, don't expect to see it as it is never put on display. However, there are numerous other important items to view here. Within the year, Atsuta Jingu hosts 60 festivals and ten religious ceremonies so there is usually something going on no matter what time you come here.

Hours:

Shrine is always open.

0900 – 1630 Treasure House

Admission Fee:

Free.

300 yen Treasure House.

How to Get Here:

1-1-1 Jingu, Atsuta-ku, Nagoya 456-8585, Aichi Prefecture. The shrine is three minutes away from Jingumae Station, five minutes from Jingunishi Station, or ten minutes away from Atsuta Station.

Nagoya-jo (Nagoya Castle)

Nagoya Castle is one of the most popular attractions in the city and is renowned for its sheer size, as well as the two golden dolphins that are situated on the top of the *donjon*, or main keep. It is located on the top of an artificial flat plain and encased by two moats. The original castle was constructed in

1612 but the building you see today dates back to 1959. Head inside the castle and explore five floors of exhibitions showcasing the history and significance of the city, as well as many hands-on exhibitions you can experience on the fifth floor. Make your way up to the top floor where you can indulge in gorgeous panoramic views over the area. Within the east gate is a traditional teahouse made from Japanese cypress trees; visitors can enjoy a traditional tea ceremony for ¥500.

Hours:

0900 – 1630 (last entry at 1600)

Admission Fee:

500 yen

How to Get Here:

1-1 Hommaru, Naka-ku, Nagoya 460-0031, Aichi Prefecture. The closest station to Nagoya Castle is Shiyakusho Station, from which it is a three-minute walk, otherwise you can take the Meguru tourist bus which costs 210 yen per ticket or 500 yen for a day pass.

Noritake Garden (Noritake-no-Mori)

If you are searching for delicate natural beauty and a serene atmosphere then pay a visit to Noritake Garden. It is here that the famous Noritake porcelain is created, its elaborate and fine colored designs being inspired by the gardens. Inside the gardens is a center where visitors can learn more about how the china is created and even get the chance to design your own piece. If you don't want to take it away with you straightaway, then they can be shipped overseas for you (but only plates at this time). The top floors feature a charming museum where you can see past works from different times. Browse other designs at the on-site shop.

Hours:

1000 to 1700 (craft center and museum)
1000 to 1800 (shops and art gallery)
1130 to 1430, 1730 to 2200 (restaurants)

Closed:

Mondays

Admission Fee:

Free.

300 yen for the craft center.

How to Get Here:

3-1-36 Noritake Shinmachi, Nishi-ku, Nagoya 451-0051, Aichi Prefecture. The garden is located 15 minutes away on foot from Nagoya Station and is on the route of the Meguru tourist bus.

Toyota Commemorative Museum of Industry and Technology (Sangyo-gijutsu Kinenkan)

The Toyota Commemorative Museum of Industry and Technology can be found within the original factory building and showcases the history of one of the world's most famous companies. Here, learn more about Toyota's textile origins and trace the history of the weaving technology before heading off to the halls to learn about their development into automobiles. The museum is ideal for kids as they can work their way through a virtual reality maze in the Technoland room, as well as lifting a 265lb engine with a handle and many other activities.

Hours:

0900 – 1700

Closed:

Mondays

Admission Fee:

500 yen

How to Get Here:

4-1-35 Noritakeshinmachi, Nishi-ku, Nagoya 451-0051, Aichi Prefecture. The museum is the first stop after Nagoya Station on the Meguru tourist bus route or it is a 20 minute walk away from the station.

Osu Kannon Temple

Located in the heart of Nagoya, the Osu Kannon Temple is a popular Buddhist temple constructed during the Kamakura Period. It was initially built in Gifu Prefecture, but was transferred to Nagoya in 1612 when the original continued to suffer damage from multiple floods. What you see today is a reconstruction dating from the 20th century.

The highlight of the temple is a beautiful wooden statue of Kannon, the Buddhist goddess of mercy, which was created by Kobo Daishi, who was a significant figure in the introduction of Buddhism to Japan. Within the Shinpukuji Library underneath the goddess' main hall is a staggering collection of 15,000 ancient Japanese and Chinese literary works, many of which have been designated as National Treasures and Important Cultural Properties. The collection also features the earliest copy of the Kojiki, which tells of the early history of Japan and its legendary beginnings.

On the 18th and 28th of every month, the temple hosts a flea market which features around 60 stalls selling everything from clothes to souvenirs.

Hours:

Always open.

Fee:

Free.

How to Get Here:

The closest train station to the temple is Osu Kannon Station.

Nightlife

Most of Nagoya's nightlife is situated close to the principal train station at the Sakae shopping area. There is a variety of restaurants, bars and clubs to enjoy and for those seeking a bit more culture, the majority of dance and musical performances can be found at the Aichi arts Center.

Elephant's Nest

The Elephant's Nest is a popular British pub in the center of the city, visited by tourists and locals alike. Sip on a variety of English ales or a pint of Guinness while watching international football on the screen or enjoy a game of darts.

How to Get Here:

2F 1-4-3 Sakae, Naka-ku, Nagoya. Tel: (052) 232 4360.

Mybar

Close to the Nagoya TV Tower, Mybar is a chic bar and restaurant catering to those who enjoy a more stylish evening. The cocktail menu is just as good as the décor and the weekly Ladies Night makes sure it's always full.

How to Get Here:

B1F 3-6-15 Nishiki, Naka-ku, Nagoya. Tel: (052) 971 8888.

Shooters Sports Bar and Grill

Situated near the Fushimi Station, Shooters Sports Bar and Grill is ideal for those who want a fun, lively atmosphere where they can enjoy a game of pool, darts, live music and great Mexican and Italian dishes.

How to Get Here:

2F Pola Building 2-9-26, Sakae, Naka-ku, Nagoya. Tel: (052) 202 7077.

iD Cafe

iD is the biggest club in the city, making it the most popular place. This is the place to be if you want to go dancing, listen to great music and enjoy a wide range of drinks. The club is spread over five floors and depending on what night you visit, the entry fee also covers the first four drinks.

How to Get Here:

Mitsukoshi Building, 3-1-15 Sakae, Naka-ku, Nagoya. Tel: (052) 251 0382.

Steps

Steps is a widely popular nightclub, especially with international visitors, which includes music, food and sports activities. It stays open until 6am and holds a pole dancing class once a week.

How to Get Here:

2F, 3-2-29 Sakae, Naka-ku, Nagoya. Tel: (052) 242 7544.

The Underground

The Underground is another popular nightclub separated into three sections where you can enjoy a range of different musical genres, including hip pop, house and soul.

How to Get Here:

Marumikanko Building 3F-4F, 4-3-15 Sakae, Naka-ku, Nagoya. Tel: (052) 242 1388.

Blue Note Nagoya

If you are a lover of jazz music then the best place to go to is Blue Note Nagoya. It is one of two jazz clubs in the city which hosts artists, both big and small, from all over Japan and the rest of the world. The restaurant serves an excellent range of dishes to enjoy with a side order of delectable music.

How to Get Here:

B2F, 3-22-20 Nishiki, Naka-ku, Nagoya. Tel: (052) 961 6311.

Gary's

For those who love R&B and Motown music, then Gary's is the ideal place for you. Many acts come all the way from the United States to play here. There is a standing area where you can enjoy drinks as you watch live performances or sit down and enjoy a meal at the restaurant as you listen.

How to Get Here:

B1F, 4-2-10 Sakae, Naka-ku, Nagoya. Tel: (052) 263 4710.

The Plastic Factory

The Plastic Factory plays a wide range of genres, everything from rock to pop, in what used to be a factory. Located in the eastern part of the city, the Plastic Factory holds various exhibitions throughout the year.

How to Get Here:

32-13 Kanda-cho, Chikusa-ku, Nagoya. Tel: (052) 723 9971.

Nagoya Noh Theater

Located within the castle grounds, Nagoya Noh Theatre holds traditional Noh performances (musical dramatic performances). The stage itself was fashioned from 600 year old cypress trees and the lighting gives performances a truly atmospheric setting.

How to Get Here:

1-1-1 Sannomaru, Naka-ku, Nagoya. Tel: (052) 231 0088.

Aichi Arts Center

Housed within the Aichi Arts Center, the Aichi Prefectural Art Theatre hosts a variety of cultural performances including classical music, ballet, contemporary dance, drama performances and occasionally traditional Japanese music, such as *koto* and *shakuhachi*.

How to Get Here:

Art Plaza, 1-13-2 Higashisakura, Higashi-ku, Nagoya. Tel: (052) 971 5511.

Where and What to Eat

Must-Try: Miso Katsu, Ankake Spaghetti, Tebasaki, Tenmusu

Budget

- Yabaton Honten Restaurant

Certain restaurants serve dishes that can match the flavor of high end ones at a quarter of a price. This one definitely is one.

- Kappa Zushi

This branch of the famous 100 yen per plate of sushi restaurant can also be found in Nagoya.

- Co-co Ichiban

This restaurant serves inexpensive Japanese curry. Most dishes are even served with a free soda.

- Spaghetti House Yokoi

Famous for the Ankake Spaghetti, this restaurant can be found in Nishiki and is a short walk from Sakae Station.

High End

- Aikyou (1-31 Nishinocho Atsuta-ku Nagoya Aichi)

This high end restaurant is just a few steps away from the central fish market where they get only the freshest seafood. You can try their *aigo nabe*, which is a stew containing a variety of exotic seafood and meat, including Nagoya chicken, Ise shrimp, Hida beef, Matsuba crab, and blowfish.

- Tower Restaurant Nagoya (460-0003 Aichi Prefecture)

Prepare to be impressed by the fancy interior and spectacular view inside this restaurant. The cuisine itself is a Japanese and European fusion.

- Garden Restaurant Tokugawaen (1001 Tokugawa-cho)

Get a taste of French-Japanese cuisine in the most glamorous restaurant in Nagoya. If you plan on eating there during spring and fall, make sure to reserve weeks ahead.

Where to Stay

Low Budget

- Nagoya B's hotel (Nagoya B's hotel 1-16-2 Nishiki, Naka-ku)

Contact number: +81 52 241 1500

This highly affordable business hotel located in the center of Nagoya offers baths and saunas. It provides guests with a free shuttle bus to and from Nagoya Station.

- Chisun Inn (1-12-8 Noritake Nakamuraku)

Contact number: +81 52 452 3211

This simple yet clean and efficient inn is great for those who do not want to spend too much for accommodations. It is also a 5-minute walk away from the train station.

- Dormy Inn Express (1-11-8 Meiekiminami, Nakamura-ku)

Guests who stay in this budget hotel often recommend it for the good food, such as the free breakfast and the midnight ramen. However, keep in mind that the communal hot bath is only open for women on weekends.

Mid-range Budget

- The Westin Nagoya Castle (3-19 Hinokuchicho, Nishi-ku)

Contact number: +81 52 521 2121

This hotel has an overall contemporary design. If you want to see the Nagoya Castle in all its splendor, you may request for a room on the higher floors.

- Meitetsu Grand Hotel (1-2-4 Meieki, Nakamura-ku)

Contact number: +81 52 582 2211

Guests find this hotel to be highly convenient as it is located right above the Nagoya Station. There is also a department store beneath it.

- Hotel MyStays Nagoya-Sakae (2-23-22 Higashi-Sakura Naka-Ku)

Contact number: +81-52-931-5811

This room offers clean and comfort at a reasonable price. It is close to the Nagoya Castle, Tokugawa Art Museum, and Nagoya City Science Museum. It is also a walk away from the Sakae shopping center and subway station.

High End

- Nagoya Kanko Hotel (1-19-30 Nishiki, Naka-ku)

Contact number: +81 52 231 7711

This classic luxury hotel is all about relaxation in utter sophistication. Look for a room with a nice view of the park.

- Hilton Nagoya (1-3-3 Sakae, Naka-ku)

Contact number: +81 52 212 1111

High end travelers never fail to mention the Hilton Hotel in Nagoya whenever they talk about excellent services and accommodations. The location makes it easy to walk to just about any destination in the city.

- Nagoya Marriott Associa Hotel (1-1-4 Meieki | Nakamura-ku, JR Central Towers Office)

Contact number: +81 52 584 1111

Business travelers will find this luxury hotel to be highly convenient because one can easily travel into and from it. Request for a room on a high floor that faces the city so you can avoid the ones facing the adjacent wall.

- ANA Crowne Plaza Hotel Grand Court Nagoya (1-1-1 Kanayamacho, Naka-ku)

Contact number: +81 52 683 4111

The Kanayama temple and the south gate of Kanayama Station are close to this high end hotel, making it easy to go to and from it as you tour around the city.

- Sir Winston Hotel (100-36 Yagoto Hon-machi, Showa-ku)

Contact number: +81 52 861 7901

This beautiful luxury hotel has the classic England interior decor. Former guests often compliment the tiny details, even right down to the charming bathtub and ample space in the powder room in your accommodations.

Conclusion

Once again thank you for choosing *Lost Travelers*!

I hope we were able to provide you with the best travel tips when visiting Japan.

And we hope you enjoy your travels.

"Travel Brings Power and Love Back to Your Life"

- Rumi

Finally, if you enjoyed this guide, then I'd like to ask you for a favor, would you be kind enough to leave a review for this book on Amazon? It'd be greatly appreciated!

- Simply search the keywords "Japan Travel Guide" on Amazon or go to our Author page "Lost Travelers" to review.

Please know that your satisfaction is important to us. If you were not happy with the book, please email us with the reason and your expectation so we may serve you more accordingly next time.

- Email: Info@losttravelers.com

Thank you and good luck!

Preview Of 'Vietnam: The Ultimate Vietnam Travel Guide By A Traveler For A Traveler

Modern-day Vietnamese trace their ancestry to the Lac people who founded a Bronze Age civilization in the first millennium BC near the fertile Red River Delta in the north. In the third century BC, a Chinese military adventurer conquered the Vietnamese kingdom of Van Lang and incorporated the Red River Delta into his expanding realm in Southern China. China eventually integrated Vietnam into its Chinese empire a hundred years later.

The more than 1,000 years of Chinese rule wrought significant changes in Vietnam's culture and society as its people were introduced to Chinese art, literature, architecture, language, ideas, religion, political system and social institutions. Ethnic Vietnamese were torn between their attraction to Chinese culture and their desire to resist the colonist's political grip. In AD 939, however, Vietnamese rebels took advantage of China's political chaos and restored national independence.

The Vietnamese Empire known as Dai Viet flourished, expanded steadily southward, and gradually formed its own institutions over a period of several hundred years. China periodically made attempts to regain control of Vietnam, but they were repulsed under the dynasty of the Ly (1000-1225AD) and the Tran (1225-1400AD). The expansion to the south continued at the expense of Champa, their southern neighbor and a civilization which flourished in South Vietnam during China's domination of the north. The Indian-influenced Champa kingdom was founded and ruled by non-Vietnamese people, the Chams.

Chinese rule was restored in the early 15th century, but a national revolt led by the Le Loi cut the reign short. This led to the formation of the Le Dynasty, which lasted from 1428 to 1788. By the 17th century, the Le Dynasty gained complete control of Southern Vietnam and ruled over the entire Mekong

River Delta. The Le leadership, however, would later slip into a civil strife between two warring royal families, the Trinh in northern Vietnam and the Nguyen in the south. The political turmoil happened at a time when European explorers were just starting to extend their missionary and commercial activities in the East, including Southeast Asia.

A peasant uprising led by the Tay Son brothers overthrew the Nguyen and the Trinh in 1771 and united the country under the leadership of the most competent among the Tay Son brothers, Emperor Nguyen Hue. His reign was short, however, as his kingdom was subdued by a military force organized by a Nguyen prince with the help of a French missionary bishop. The victory ushered in the Nguyen Dynasty (1802-1945) and reunified the country under the leadership of Emperor Gia Long. The alliance between France and the Nguyen dynasty, however, soon turned sour as both Gia Long and his son and successor, Minh Mang, refused to grant missionary and commercial privileges to France. TO BE CONTINUED!

Check out the rest of Vietnam: The Ultimate Vietnam Travel Guide on Amazon by simply searching it.

Check Out Our Other Guides

Below you'll find some of our other popular books that are on Amazon and Kindle as well. Simply search the titles below to check them out. Alternatively, you can visit our author page (Lost Travelers) on Amazon to see other work done by us.

- Vienna: The Ultimate Vienna Travel Guide By A Traveler For A Traveler

- Barcelona: The Ultimate Barcelona Travel Guide By A Traveler For A Traveler

- London: The Ultimate London Travel Guide By A Traveler For A Traveler

- Istanbul: The Ultimate Istanbul Travel Guide By A Traveler For A Traveler

- Vietnam: The Ultimate Vietnam Travel Guide By A Traveler For A Traveler

- Peru: The Ultimate Peru Travel Guide By A Traveler For A Traveler

- Australia: The Ultimate Australia Guide By A Traveler For A Traveler

- New Zealand: The Ultimate New Zealand Travel Guide By A Traveler For A Traveler

- Dublin: The Ultimate Dublin Travel Guide By A Traveler For A Traveler

- Thailand: The Ultimate Thailand Travel Guide By A Traveler For A Traveler

- Iceland: The Ultimate Iceland Travel Guide By A Traveler For A Traveler

- Santorini: The Ultimate Santorini Travel Guide By A Traveler For A Traveler

- Italy: The Ultimate Italy Travel Guide By A Traveler For A Traveler

You can simply search for these titles on the Amazon website to find them.

Made in the USA
Las Vegas, NV
15 February 2025

18194596R00075